Three Boys

RITA TROTMAN

First Published in Great Britain in 2013 as
Sunlight Through The Shadows

In memory of Didi Rotaru

1946 - 2019

Diary entry North East Romania May 29th 1991
The Camine in Giurcani

I am lying on a mattress puddled with stains. A rolled-up jacket is masquerading as my pillow and only a sleeping bag lies between my skin and a stranger's long-dried, bodily fluids. Sleep is hampered by the cloying heat; I'm moistened to a distasteful sheen and mosquitos are feasting on my delicate parts. My nostrils are colonised by the stench of human deprivation.

My room is dark as only rural habitation can be. There is no electricity, no necklace of streetlights and no hum of traffic. As I toss and turn, I see images of chocolate-eyed children with matchstick arms, reaching out for love. I am drowning in their sea of hopelessness and do not have the capacity to love them all.

A scream of agonised terror disturbs me. I lie still and take deep breaths to calm my heartbeat, but fear dampens my palms. Another harrowing scream, this one is shorter and muffled, and even more terrifying. I can forgive that I am afraid, but failure to make a difference is not an option.

I have surely arrived in hell.

'I never expected anyone to rescue me 'cos there was nowhere to go, that I knew of. We just had to manage. Nobody had enough food and we all got beaten. It's how things were.'

Gheorgie – a survivor of the camine in Giurcani

Chapter 1

What makes a good volunteer? Who zips across Europe on a whim to help stricken children? It is not an easy question to answer. A foolish person, perhaps? An interfering do-gooder? I guess the answer could be an enthusiastic amateur, and I like to think I sat firmly in that camp.

When entering a country that has been closed to visitors for forty years and about which little is known, warning bells should sound. But if they rang, I didn't hear them. I undertook a crazy mission with a low chance of success, but I wouldn't have done it any other way.

My journey was instigated by a television programme called *Challenge Anneka* which documented a mercy-mission to a Romanian orphanage. What viewers saw one winter night in nineteen ninety, reverberated around the country, and for some a deep anger burned into an unquenchable fire. Viewers watched in horror as the conditions within the camine (orphanage) were exposed, and that bombshell insight was a pivotal moment in my life.

It was the images of small children with huge eyes and malnourished bodies that lingered. All attempts to jettison them were fruitless and Romania became an irritable fly that refused to be squashed. I knew I couldn't turn my back on the cruelty and deprivation I'd witnessed, and although my response was ill thought out and impulsive, I turned that impulse into action; I knew instantly I was going to Romania to help.

Just by chance, and through a convoluted series of telephone calls, I made contact with Jane Clarke who had already instigated a group of Marks and Spencer's employees to take an aid lorry across Europe to a village called Giurcani. On their return, they were looking for volunteers to offer hands-on work with the children. Tailor made for me, I decided.

I'd like to say I used my maturity to make an informed decision, but the truth was, I neither looked at an atlas nor researched the country or its politics. Imploring eyes and skinny torsos drove me with an urgency my friends found hard to comprehend. I was prepared to take a chance and determined to make a difference.

The following May I agreed to trace the footsteps of Marks and Spencer to the village of Giurcani. Jane Clarke promised an English-speaking Romanian would meet me at Bucharest airport and take me to the camine. She added that tinned food had been left in the village in the hope that others would follow. Information was scant, but I knew not to expect a telephone connection or safe drinking water. I would have to organise my own regime within the camine.

My beloved, mostly grown-up sons James and Robert have always been the centre point of my life. They are my *raison d'etre*. Both were busy at that time with their own lives and when I shared my intention, they gave me big hugs and told me to take care. They were supportive, but I suspect there were eyes raised to heaven at yet another of Mother's hairbrained schemes. I was confident I had raised sensible lads and had no need to worry about them. Friends offered to act as anchors on my behalf, and so I prepared for my departure.

I bought an air ticket to Bucharest. Could I achieve anything worthwhile in three months? I had no idea, but I had to try. Crying about television images was an understandable, immediate response, but not a productive one - certainly not for those children.

I wasn't looking for that eureka moment in my life although, over the years, I've met a few volunteers who were. For me, this trip was an adventure, albeit one driven by genuine concern. I felt an urge to do something worthwhile, but only intended to do what was possible in the short time I'd allotted myself. Maybe there is something about your mid-forties that defines the DNA of your life. I was old enough to trust my instincts, young enough to think I was indestructible and freed from the responsibility of young children. Sounded like heaven!

I had recently sold a business and had a three-month window to do something useful. If enthusiasm and resourcefulness were requirements, then I possessed them in bucket loads. With a nursing background and being the mother of boys who had made it to adulthood, mostly unscathed, I felt qualified – or as qualified as anyone else was likely to be.

My flight was delayed at Heathrow and I refused to consider the consequences if my Romanian contact had scarpered. In nineteen ninety-one it was difficult for foreigners to check into a Romanian hotel and, as I was to learn, there were few hotels anyone would want to sleep in.

When the flight eventually landed in Bucharest, the heat and excitement enveloped me as I stepped onto Romanian soil. The crowd was a shifting human mass which gave me no choice but to follow. Everything was dilapidated, unfamiliar and dirty and no one smiled. At baggage reclaim I was particularly anxious; would there be any luggage to collect? Theft was to be expected, I had been reliably informed.

High-up in the corrugated roof, shards of sunlight were hampered by grimy windows. Litter soiled the floors and everywhere had the charm of a concentration camp. But most alarming were the uniformed staff with faces like undertakers. They lurked around every corner, equipped with large guns which they looked more than capable of using.

I forged my way through grubby, unpainted corridors to find the visa department. There was no queuing system, just a push and shove regime which astounded the Britishness in me. Always quick to learn, I joined the crowd of excitable people and exercised my elbows to good effect.

I needed an entry visa which cost the exorbitant sum of fifty US dollars and while waiting for the date stamping and paper shuffling, I remember feeling grumpy at the exorbitant cost. Officialdom is inbred in Romanians – nurtured by the rule of Ceausescu and Communism. Many times, I have been heard to mutter about awarding a 'jobsworth cap' to surly government workers who would rather impede your progress than help. Happily, there are fewer year on year, and they are more than compensated for by the warm Romanians who have offered me kindness.

After an age of waiting, my rucksack appeared on the conveyor belt, sandwiched between black bin liners of stuff, parcels tied with string and battered suitcases. My relief was palpable when I retrieved my worldly goods and heaved them onto my back. I was a rucksack rookie and there was a knack I hadn't yet grasped for dealing with the weight. Amongst my flea-brain thoughts, I feared falling over, fully laden like a stranded sheep on its back, unable to right itself. I also imagined the public humiliation it would cause.

Some two and a half hours late, I emerged intact into the meet and greet area with not only my luggage and a visa, but a few lei acquired at a currency exchange. In nineteen ninety-one the exchange rate was 325 lei to the dollar. I was a millionaire!

'I had a value, you see. I was a good worker, and I hoed the fields and washed clothes until I was so tired, I could hardly stand up. Sometimes my food was eaten by someone else.'
  Adrian – a survivor of the camine in Giurcani

I need not have worried about being abandoned in Bucharest for I was met, as promised, by a patient young Romanian called Renato. He held up a placard on which my name loomed large and after smiles and introductions, this slim Latino with a ponytail made his way to the airport exit. I followed.

The terminal was a heaving throng. Walnut-skinned, Romany gypsies drifted around in bunches of eight or ten, many had papoose-style attachments from which

5

small, black-haired babies poked their heads. The women were unsmiling and looked on with black, searching eyes. They wore multi-coloured skirts, gathered at the waist, which swished around their ankles. Tight bodices, laced at the front, flaunted ample supplies of womanly charm.

Renato told me to take care of my valuables as theft was commonplace and the women, he explained, were experts. The Romanies floated like Amazonian parrots, eyeing the crowds and looking for someone careless with their belongings. They surely perceived me as an exciting prospect. I followed Renato, rarely taking my eyes off him for fear of being lost in a hostile world. I was mesmerised by all the activity.

Eventually we arrived outside where the evening heat slammed me like a blanket of fire. Here, even more chaos danced around, mostly in the form of vociferous taxi drivers touting for fares, indolent gypsy men smoking and drinking from beer bottles, and everyday working people hurrying about their business. There was the general bustle of travellers, as seen in any capital city in the world, but it was the poverty that was impossible to ignore. Tatty clothes, children without shoes and rust-bucket cars. Everything shouted of deprivation which astounded me in a European country. Heavy pollution thickened the air and created a hazy sunlight.

Doubts washed over me. Fears about my ability to cope with what lay ahead and that twenty-million-dollar question – had I bitten off more that I could chew? Renato explained that members of his family were waiting to meet me as they had never met a foreign person. And within seconds, as if by magic, his father and younger brother appeared with big smiles and outstretched hands. They were clearly curious about a western woman heaving her worldly goods around in a rucksack. Over the coming days I would notice how I stood out from the crowd. And not in a good way. I might as well have carried a placard saying *'foreigner'*.

We took a taxi from the queue of eager drivers. My luggage was stowed in the boot and we squeezed into an old Dacia car. My knees were under my chin while the car coughed and spluttered its way off the airport concourse. I craned my neck to take a first glimpse of the city which looked very 'Iron Curtain' and exciting, if a little grim.

Renato told me we would travel via Ceausescu's Palace, a building of much renown. Even as a seasoned traveller I was astounded by the size and grandeur of it – *'twenty-six football pitches long'*, I was proudly informed. How could a man live in such opulence yet allow Romania's people to live in abject poverty? The palace was legendary among the people. No wonder they shot him.

After duly admiring the palace, we stepped from the taxi next to an ugly tenement building. Cars hooted and people stared amongst the choking pollution. The buildings were no better than slum tenement blocks. In fact, I was askance that people lived in them. The deep orange sun had already set behind the skyline although the cloying heat clung like a limpet. I was desperate to shed my rucksack and have a wash.

But there were problems ahead. To reach our accommodation we needed to climb eight flights of concrete stairs as, sadly for me, a notice confirmed the lift was 'waiting for repair.' Renato apologised and said it had been broken for more than six months. There were few lights to show the way and we trudged ever upwards in semi-darkness. When I asked about the lack of illumination, Renato was unsure if the light bulbs were broken, or the electricity was switched off – either way we had to watch our footing on the crumbling steps. The ever-increasing strain of my rucksack niggled as I attacked more than fifty steps at the grand age of forty-four. But I took heart, knowing the next day it would all be downhill!

Renato's cousin was a lovely man with two adult daughters called Dorothea and Nina. I was welcomed into a sparsely furnished home of which they were clearly proud. Nina spoke a little English and was fascinated to know about my life. Did everyone have a colour television? Did we all have jobs and plenty to eat? Did we go to the coast for our holidays? Dorothea was shy and had little to say, but she was interested in everything Renato translated. I had a supper of boiled eggs, hard cheese, bread and coffee and the girls waited on table as I ate alone. It felt strange, but I would become familiar with the custom.

The apartment boasted an indoor bathroom with flushing loo. I washed and changed into pyjamas and fell, exhausted into bed. The following day it was more eggs and bread and when I used the bathroom again, little did I realise this would be the last running water I would enjoy for some time.

Renato and I made our way to the railway station by tram, accompanied by Dorothea and Nina. I could sense their interest in my clothes, hair and shoes and they surely thought me a strange specimen from the west. I was beginning to feel the odd ball amongst the hundreds of locals who took it in turns to stare at me with unbridled interest.

Paying for the tickets was my first battle with lei, the value of which has always remained a mystery to me, (particularly after it was devalued in the late nineties.) I pushed a wad of 'Monopoly' money into Renato's hand as he explained not all trains had first class carriages, but he was hopeful we would be lucky. We were indeed lucky and for what felt like a pittance, we purchased first class tickets to Birlad for our seven-hour journey. From Birlad we would take a pre-arranged car ride to the village of Giurcani which would take another hour.

I asked Renato how many lei would be appropriate to thank my hosts and duly paid Nina and Dorothea for my accommodation and food. I said goodbye and thanked the first Romanian family of my acquaintance for their hospitality and kindness. I'd left chocolate for them by my bed, and I hoped I'd see them again one day, although I never did.

It was time to join the throng of people bustling to catch their trains. I struggled to climb aboard ours via particularly high, wide metal steps and needed a helping hand to heave the rucksack on to the train. And at precisely eight-thirty, not a minute early and not a minute late, the train left the station with much whistleblowing, waving and shouting from a uniformed guard, resplendent in peaked cap and navy and scarlet tunic. I had my nose glued to the window, mesmerised by the sights.

As we pulled away, I witnessed a scene resembling a film-set in Russia at the turn of the nineteenth century.

People were scattered like ants; porters in uniform balanced piles of luggage on carts and mothers pulled at small children, urging them to keep up. The screech of traditional Romanian music bellowed from loudspeakers and assaulted the ears while the smell of burnt diesel oil and hot metal filled my nostrils. Children munched popcorn and the ubiquitous gypsies were scattered like jewels across the grey concrete station.

When travelling on a gasping, communist train, the Romanian village of Giurcani is eight long hours from Bucharest. Hour upon exhausting hour I stared from a railway carriage window and pondered my fate for the coming months.

I loved the comfort of our plush, first class carriage with its large window and netted luggage racks. Renato read a book while I alternated reading and sleeping until eventually, I strayed into other carriages to stretch my legs. I exchanged smiles with dozens of down-trodden individuals. Some guarded chickens in cages, others seeped suspicion over me, worried that I would take their meagre parcels of food. All stared in amazement at a smiling, middle-aged English woman in shorts and a 'Queen's Concert' tee shirt. I could have landed from Mars.

I grasped the significance of second-class travel. The benches were built of bare wood and were graced by an incongruous array of people. Many seats were shared with livestock. Two ducks in a cage made a fearful noise and I spotted chickens held in laps, including a ferocious cockerel under a blanket. And the travellers were as interested in me as I in them. When I mentioned to Renato I'd caused some stares, he laughed and told me, *'You had better get used to it. Villagers will be fascinated by you - they'll want to know how old you are, where is your husband and why don't you wear a skirt and headscarf?' Hmm* …

I survived the journey despite the heat, the persistent sullen gypsy women selling black sunflower seeds for snacking, and the agonising slowness of the train. I even survived the lavatory which consisted of a cubicle where a hole exposed the scary, moving train track. The entire floor was covered in excrement. I felt very brave.

The train lingered at dozens of small stations, most having a concrete slab of platform on which a small hut served as the ticket office. Travellers jumped off and filled plastic bottles with water from grubby fountains, before boarding again as the whistle-blowing guard sent us on our way. Shouts, salutations and laughter floated on the air as people alighted to make their way home.

When the train stopped in a rush of steam in Birlad station, a demented uniformed man charged up and down the train blowing his whistle and urging those who were leaving to hurry along. And shockingly, we had to step straight on to a railway track. Alighting from a train without a platform, according to Renato, was not unusual and he assured me the lines were not 'live'. So, it wasn't all bad news! We crossed two more pairs of tracks to reach the station platform and it was very scary. Luckily, no distant locomotive could be heard bearing down on us from either direction.

Although we had arrived at Birlad, we still had another hour of travel eastwards before reaching

Giurcani. Miraculously, the promised man with a car introduced himself and we were whisked through the busy streets in another battered Dacia. I thought to myself – Giurcani, are you ready for me?

Chapter 2

*'Umm.....I've been treated badly you know.
People used to kick me when I was young. I
could never get things right, you see.'*

Gheorgie – a survivor of the camine in Giurcani

Our car journey followed in the footsteps of the Marks
and Spencer team; we whizzed through two-bit towns
and villages and endless miles of open plain without a
tree in sight. I felt we were travelling to the ends of the
earth. I was hungry and tired and dozed a little while
Renato kept up a conversation with the driver. I tried
not to dwell on what lay ahead.

When we finally arrived, I saw what looked like an
isolated outpost in which I guessed, a community
dredged up an existence. The road sign told me it was
Giurcani. It was one of the most easterly villages of
Europe and just three miles from the Russian border.
(Later, after the break-up of Russia, Romania's near
neighbour would be the country of Moldova.)

Giurcani is situated two hours south of the university
city of Iasi and the village, small by any standards, could
not object to being labelled a rural backwater. Many
inhabitants had never been more than twenty miles
from the village.

My curious eyes were met with one long dirt road
with winding, narrow pathways that disappeared at

regular intervals. Single storey, rusty, tin-roofed houses were scattered like pebbles across a desolate land. Ducks and geese waddled the length and breadth of the village and drank from the storm gullies that stretched along the roadside. Skinny children peeped from behind stark metal fences and stacks of hay.

In was early summer and dust from the unmade road swirled unmercifully around every living thing. The regular comings and goings of horses and carts lifted swathes of dust into eyes and settled grit between toes. Flies tormented and mosquitoes bit. I was told, when the rains came, they were monsoon-like and ruthless, and the entire village became a bath of thick, sticky mud. Renato said that in winter the road was impassable. Mountains of snow often blocked the village for weeks.

Renato instructed the driver to stop at a house mid-way down the main street and his extended family appeared to welcome us. I entered their garden through a wrought iron gate which yielded to a concrete path. A family group watched me with curious eyes as I was introduced to the lovely people who would host me for the foreseeable future. I was told Renato's Aunt Johanna worked at the camine as a seamstress but her husband, Costel, did not appear to have a job.

The home was clean and welcoming. Religious icons of the Russian Orthodox persuasion stared down from the walls and evidence of Johanna's artistic talent was everywhere. Crocheted armrests to the chairs, embroidered pictures, rag rugs to the floors - I admired a myriad of colourful items in my new, temporary home.

The house had two kitchens which mimicked every other house in the village. One kitchen was indoors for cooking in deepest winter and the other, larger one, was outside and used for fine weather cooking. It also served as the preparation and bottling area for the fruits of the summer harvest. It was from one of those kitchens a feast appeared, and it met with two enthusiastic diners.

The washing facility was outdoors in the back yard and consisted of a plastic water container set above an incongruous porcelain basin. A shelf held the family toothbrushes and there was a mirror to check hair and makeup. I sensed privacy was going to be sparce for the coming months.

Johanna was a quiet slip of a woman with sad, deep brown eyes. She made me welcome in her home and nothing was too much trouble. Sadly, within three years her life was claimed by cancer. Shockingly, I discovered that no medicine was available unless the families had money to pay for it.

Johanna and Costel had two teenage daughters and a son living at home. As with all young people in Romania, they were desperate to learn English and hung on my every word about life in the west. Without a common language, I managed to build a relationship with that lovely family and happily exchanged English lessons for help with Romanian vocabulary. I'd brought an English/Romanian dictionary which was the starting point for many amusing language sessions.

I slept in a clean bed and ate sufficient, if not sophisticated food. As I had been pre-warned that the water was unsafe, I'd brought a compact water purifying system, consisting of a bottle with a charcoal filter. (This item proved invaluable as many people died of water-borne diseases in Giurcani.) But my caution about the water supply caused the host family some amusement. They could not understand what I was doing and – well, have you ever tried to explain water purification via a game of charades!

Renato wanted me to meet the camine director while he was around to translate for us and I was keen to meet her, too. Rumour suggested she was a lady of some repute, but thankfully, she was expecting my arrival. Johanna told me the head honcho had declared that she had *'no idea what foreigners were going to do in her camine or how long they intended to stay.'* I feared that attitude did not bode well.

The next day Renato and I walked along the village road towards the camine and created a huge amount of interest. Royalty could not have received a better welcome. Little girls came out of gateways with bunches of wildflowers and a couple of people offered me hospitality of the alcoholic variety. Renato kindly refused on my behalf. He explained I was tired after a long journey the day before, but I would call to see them another day. Over the years, I received hospitality and generosity inside those village houses that moved me greatly. Although Romanian people have little, they are incredibly generous with what they have.

The Russian Orthodox Church, which stole the skyline played a significant role in the ebb and flow of village life. Weddings, Saints' Days, Easter, Christmas, christenings, and funerals all played their part within the life cycle of the people. And, one supposes, the forgiveness of sins.

The camine was easy to spot as it sat like a carbuncle with a dark, dark secret. Surrounded by spiked fencing which gathered to meet an enormous metal gate, I never decided if it was keeping people in, or keeping people out. It was surrounded by acres of cultivated land. I saw waving corn and wheat ripening in the sun and fruit trees fat with promise.

My curious eyes spotted a small farm on the outer limits of the land with outbuildings, pig pens and at least one cow. A couple of dogs yapped a warning and one, I remember, had a penchant for ankles. The camine horse was tethered in the heat, fully harnessed and without an ounce of fat on its puny, sweating body. It was swatting big, fat flies with its tail and its head hung in abject misery.

The camine was huge by village standards with dozens of boarded-up windows and one end wrapped inside a glass conservatory. An attempt had been made to create a flowerbed, but no essence of any living thing was visible. Everything was tired, crumpled and overdue for a face-lift, which wasn't coming in the foreseeable future.

We were met by a group of teenaged boys who jabbered excitedly as they bumbled down the dusty track towards us. I had a pocket full of sweets which they relieved me of in double quick time. Renato was in constant conversation with them, presumably explaining all about the strange foreign visitor.

We entered the camine through French double doors and my heart was racing, my mouth dry. The older boys coaxed and cajoled me to step inside while doubt was up to her tricks. What had I done? Why was I there? Hesitantly, I batted aside the filthy net curtains and stepped into a dark corridor. My stomach began to flutter as the first whiff of deprivation assaulted my nostrils. Inside, I was met with stone walls, stone floors and a stench that had me reaching for my handkerchief. Seventy unwanted children were living like festering bugs on a laboratory bench. I felt insignificant and afraid, but remembered I was there to help.

The stone floor was under assault from a mop and bucket wielded by a tall, sullen boy. He slopped copious amounts of water around which he then retrieved with his mop. He oozed the fetid water through a plastic grid into his bucket and gave his plastic sandals a shower for good measure. I remember thinking he was more man than child and wondered if he was a member of staff or one of the children.

I was met in the corridor by two enthusiastic girls. One wore a red tartan skirt with just a ragged vest and bare feet. She limped and dragged her left leg behind her, but my eyes were drawn to her beaming smile. The other, slightly older girl was naked, and blood ran down her legs. She had her period but no apparent means of dealing with it. Her distended stomach reminded me of starving children I'd seen in documentaries. My heart went out to these girls.

A scruffy, blond boy with bright blue eyes, probably aged about thirteen I guessed, urged me further inside while the boy with the mop and bucket pushed past me to empty its content outside. He chucked the water against the wall of the building where it stained the dreary grey to a suspect brown before it ran in rivulets across the weather-bitten concrete path. The smell was 'sewage special.' As I took another couple of steps into the camine, the stench of human misery choked me. A blonde boy, Adrian, beckoned me to turn left along a further corridor into the dining-room; he coaxed me forward with his light bulb smile.

Suddenly, members of staff made an appearance. Women dressed in blue overalls and white headscarves, all with deeply wrinkled faces, stared at me. It was hard to define their ages as life had clearly taken its toll. They, too, were curious and chattered among themselves, speculating, maybe, about this strange foreign woman dressed in shorts and a T- shirt.

I noticed dented, metal dishes and twisted spoons stacked on a shelf. Through the serving-hatch I caught a glimpse of the kitchen. I wondered how seventy children could be fed in that small dining-room; the answer to many of my questions would soon become apparent. I was to learn that only the strongest and able-bodied children made it to the dining room at mealtimes. The others had alternative methods of feeding which I would soon be campaigning to change.

One side of the room was filled with a typical Romanian stove. Brown, high–gloss tiles created the only source of winter heat and covered a large proportion of the wall from ceiling to floor. I noticed an incongruous light-fitting which was madly off-centre and had only one lightbulb where there should be eight. Grubby net curtains covered the windows and apart from utilitarian tables and benches, there was nothing else in the room.

More children came to inspect me, and the noise level rose. Suddenly, due to a shout and much jabbering, I became aware that another boy had arrived from outside. I was reliably informed he was called

Dorin. He looked about fifteen and had major physical challenges. At first glance he appeared to have no hands or feet, but closer inspection showed he had a thumb on each elbow, and he lacked the long bones in his legs. He had twisted stumps for feet which gave his short stature a pronounced shambling walk. But he was handsome and dynamic and clearly annoyed that he'd missed my arrival. He scattered what I thought was a myriad of questions in my direction, clearly unable to grasp that I couldn't understand a word he said. This boy had eyes like melting toffee, and they sparkled with more life than I imagined could exist in such a place. Banter broke out between Dorin and the staff and I sensed he was liked by everyone. He was a breath of fresh air in that fetid environment.

When I entered the living block proper, it was taste rather than smell that further assaulted me. So thick was the stench of human excrement hanging on the warm air, that a reflex action sent one hand to my nose while the other scrabbled for a handkerchief. My fixed smile slipped to somewhere around my churning stomach.

The older children, delighted with my arrival, encouraged me deeper into the dark, unwelcoming passageways. They jabbered and beckoned for me to follow them into the rooms beyond. A lad called Gheorgie took my hand to ensure I didn't make an escape. How intuitive was that boy? He had conjunctivitis in both eyes, and I wondered if he had received treatment and how many other children he'd infected.

I hadn't experienced fear since I was a child, but this place instilled it in bucket loads. A sense of self-preservation and my sweaty palms told me to get out as I advanced down the corridor. But my passion to help the children gave me a good slap on the wrist. Failing at the first hurdle was not an option.

I walked deeper into the gloom and remember stepping over piles of excrement casually deposited in the passageway. There was an eerie silence lying beyond the three excited boys who led the way. Other children and the chattering staff brought up the rear. It was hard to believe more than seventy children were incarcerated in that place. Where were they all? How had they not died of disease? Time would reveal the answers to all my questions, but nothing would ever rinse the memory of that initial visit from my mind.

On entering one of the salons, I found toddlers in blacked-out rooms. When I peered into the gloom, I discovered two little bodies in each rusting cot or bed. Slowly, as my eyes adjusted, I could make out shapes on filthy mattresses while some lay on bare wire springs. Babies vied for space with piles of poo on the sodden sheets. There was not a whimper from any of them. Some, those able to sit, rocked gently without turning their eyes in my direction. Their interest in the world had long been obliterated. Skin, the colour of milk, covered spindle-limbs and most were too weak to support their body weight. Some of them wore clothes but everything was soiled. For the naked ones, shivers suggested cold had seeped into their little bodies, even on a warm day in May. Nothing penetrated the rooms except the smell of poverty and neglect. I'd seen better conditions in cowsheds.

When Adrian, Dorin and Gheorgie beckoned me into their world, it was a monumental moment in my life. They were spotty adolescents with none of the charm of the younger children in the camine, those who readily won people's hearts. But to me, those teenage boys were special. They were scruffy and shy and probably perplexed that anyone would want to be nice to them after a lifetime of neglect. And yes, rather smelly, too.

For all western visitors, the camine in Giurcani was a surreal experience. There was a division of children and it didn't take long to see why. At first, I noticed the older, skinny, and under-developed boys appeared to work outside on the land. Then there were smaller, mobile children who never went outside, but appeared to spend their days in the salons surrounded by the excrement and neglect. Lastly, there were the sickly, undernourished of all ages who lingered in cots and beds. Many of the latter were tied down with strips of sheeting or had their hands secured behind their backs. It was a shocking sight. All were needy beyond comprehension, but it was the younger children, those who were too weak to leave their beds, who caught most attention. They were a tangle of thin arms and legs and gaunt faces reminiscent of images of the Holocaust.

All the children in the camine had physical or mental disabilities. Many had weeping sores, impetigo, which was roughly daubed with gentian violet, and an array of bruises obtained, one assumed, from unfettered violence. I came to realise that very few ills or ailments were ever treated. Boils were left to their own devices, eventually bursting their putrid content, but there was no means of dressing the wound. Toothache was rarely mentioned as it was an inherent part of the regime and must be borne until pain prevented the child from eating or working. Then expense would grudgingly be spared to take the child to the dentist. No money was available for an anaesthetic, under any circumstances.

Most windows in the salons were boarded over to prevent any advantage from sunlight or fresh air. The stench throughout the building was a living thing that crept along the floors, working its way into every nook and cranny and every pore of your body. Instead of care and nurture these children endured incarceration, starvation and deprivation. They knew no human touch or kindness, had no one to trust and no one to protect them. They were deprived of everything a child needs to grow and flourish. And the greatest shock of all for me – the staff appeared to think camine-life was normal.

My introduction to the camine director was a rather starchy event. She was a good-looking woman with a ready shrug about most things I asked Renato to translate. Supplying sufficient food for the children was a problem, finding good staff was a problem and keeping the children clean and stimulated was a foreign language to her. I knew there were mountains to climb. I had hopes that the deputy director would be more pleasant to deal with, and as it turned out, it was a good assumption. Lena was my saving grace on many occasions, and we became friends over the years.

Although most of my early working days were spent with the small children, it was three of the oldest boys who shaped my long-term commitment to Giurcani. Adrian, Dorin and Gheorgie were the subject of many of my diary entries and I want to tell their story to the world, as they told it to me or as I witnessed it during my visits to Giurcani. Those lads were uneducated, hard-working, and bullied and, as I discovered much later, they all had families somewhere in Romania. I witnessed, first-hand, a raw example of child slavery. They grew up in the camine as close as brothers, always looking out for each other. Their two main enemies were hunger and cruelty and they shielded each other from both, the best way they could. Unusually for camine children they had two things in common; firstly, they were brave enough to dream of a better life, and secondly, they knew who might achieve it for them. I like to believe that from my very first visit they knew my affection was genuine. They were special human beings and gifted me, and later my husband, with their trust. We would not let them down.

I think the most important lesson I absorbed in the camine was never to judge before looking at the details of a situation. It was easy to be a harsh critic when the true horrors of the camine revealed themselves, but as I quickly learned, there is always another point of view.

I developed empathy for the staff. They were village women living in abject poverty, doing their best to earn a pittance to keep their families afloat. Often, they were the sole breadwinner, and many had an alcoholic husband to contend with. It was easy to criticise anyone who allowed children to live in squalor, but one had to balance that view against poverty and the indoctrination of a dictator who had insisted disability must be hidden from the world. I had been told much about Ceausescu, but I was yet to learn about the tyrant camine director, she who scared the women witless and

24

ruled with iron discipline. She did not scare me but she quickly became a challenge.

My first visit to Giurcani was sixteen months after the Romanian people shot Ceausescu and communism still loomed large. The villagers, however, sniffed the tantalising fragrance of western culture on an English woman, and some days I felt guilty about my privileged existence. Inbred fear of strangers was the villager's dominant emotion around me - they wondered what I wanted. Why had I arrived in their village with my strange looks and unintelligible language? They could sense wealth and good fortune around me at a time when their longing for a new life was already fading. They were resigned to a continued life of hardship, for the post-Ceausescu government had already trampled on their dreams. I could see it written all over their weary faces.

Village life in nineteen ninety-one was tough. High unemployment made it difficult to provide even the basics of life for their families and left little enthusiasm or energy to show concern for orphans. (A euphemism, of course, as most of those children in the camine weren't orphans.) Camine children were simply being punished for their disabilities or because their parents were too poor to keep them. Only a few were punished because their parents were inconsiderate enough to die while they were young.

Village women who worked in the camine were indoctrinated to believe disability was a shame, a scar on society. They believed such children to be the responsibility of the State and they were no more than a source of essential income.

Chapter 3

'I shared my bed with someone who never seemed to sleep. Sometimes he wet himself and I woke up covered in his pee.'

Gheorgie – a survivor of the camine in Giurcani

I continued to live with the lovely village family who fed me and helped me learn Romanian. Many happy evenings were spent in the sunshine combining laughter and local wine over stumbling vocabulary. But there was trouble ahead. It was to be the first of many power struggles I would have with the director of the camine. On this occasion, she won.

At the end of the fourth week the director called me into her office. We'd had a couple of spats, communicated in a mixture of French and Romanian, and always about the treatment of the children. On this occasion, however, I deduced I could no longer stay with my host family in the village. They were, to quote her words, *'not important enough to have a foreigner staying with them.'* As Johanna was a member of staff at the camine it was tricky to object, for I feared there may be reprisals for her if I disobeyed. Could she even lose her job, I wondered?

I suspected there was jealousy afoot. I was paying generously for my board and lodgings and this put the family at an advantage, compared to everyone else in the village. Stupidly, as it turned out, I allowed myself to be ordered to live in the camine where I was shown to a small, dark side-room and told this was my accommodation for the foreseeable future.

Maybe the director thought the conditions would get rid of me – perhaps she thought they would send me back to England with my tail between my legs. Maybe it was the hope of rent money, who knew? The allotted room, which was used as a sewing room by Johanna during the daytime, had two single beds of camine quality and smell, a sewing machine on a table, a chair and very little else. I dumped my rucksack on the floor which looked cleaner than the beds and asked myself, yet again, what had I done?

I tried to open the shutters which boarded the filthy window but was rebuked by Queen Bee. So, small, dark, smelly and soulless was the full extent of what appeared to be my new living space. Gone was the family welcome and reasonable food and I knew I'd miss the friendship of the lovely Ursu family. I curled up inside my sleeping bag to contemplate the future.

I witnessed atrocities in the camine that I could never commit to print, but the *'happening in the night'* is embedded in my DNA. Those afore mentioned screams of terror have never left me and the determination to make a tangible difference for at least some of those children, was probably born that night.

The evening they occurred had been unremarkable. I'd crept outside the camine to wash as usual. I'd closed the door to my room and walked along corridors as black as treacle with my trusty torch which I'd quickly learned was my new, best friend. When I stepped outside, I welcomed the light spring evening and the freshness of cut grass on the air mingled with musk from the horse, which I knew was tethered nearby. I recognised the gentle chomping of the camine's cow as she shuffled from one meagre, weedy tuft to the next, somewhere beyond the chain-linked fencing. An owl called to its mate - an oddly comforting sound of home.

There had been a heavy shower earlier and I slid on a topcoat of mud. It was greasy and black and squelched between toes and caked my sandals. It had an unfamiliar odour. A bucket hung from a nail in the wall, the content of which was my makeshift bathroom. A layer of scum on the surface was no doubt the remnants of someone else's ablutions, and it reminded me of cow troughs at home. I unzipped my wash bag, balanced it on the kitchen window-ledge and found the basic necessities inside. I couldn't raise a lather from my scented soap but held the fragrant tablet to my nose while thoughts of home nudged me, seeking out a soft spot to torment. I fought the emotion; it was almost too much to bear. I thought of bathrooms, flushing loos, running water and my sons who were as likely to be ensconced in the pub with friends, as in their warm beds.

I wasted no time and after a token wash, gathered my belongings and retraced my steps. My unattended room concerned me, for the loss of possessions at that point would have been disastrous. My Walkman and books were precious and as far as I could tell, this land was devoid of material items. With long hours to fill, I dreaded finding paperbacks chewed or my passport ripped to shreds, for how would I ever get home?

As I returned to my room, I met several children who should have been in bed. They giggled and chattered and disappeared from the beam of my torch. And then I witnessed two small boys, dressed only in T- shirts, peering through the keyhole to my room. They were surely a couple of moments away from entering. Thieving comes easily to those who have nothing, particularly when you're starving, beaten and unloved. I shooed them away gently and watched them scamper down the corridor. Their little bodies disappeared into the black of the night.

And then, when I was curled-up inside my sleeping bag, came those screams of terror from somewhere nearby. High pitched and regular, they became rhythmic and accompanied by deep, guttural breathing. The sickening cries filled a dark space and only an insignificant wall lay between us.

I knew it was human suffering. No fox on heat ever attained such decibels and my senses defined it, not from personal experience, but some primeval essence that welled up and named it for me. It was true fear. Not the horror movie kind, not the being chased by baddies type; this brand of fear created a curdling of acid rather too low-down for comfort. I snatched a breath, seeking oxygen from the frugal air which gave nothing but the stench of human suffering. I hadn't signed up for this. Nothing in my past life had prepared me for this.

I heard children's voices from all directions and then a repeat of those blood-curdling screams. There was a consistent sound of children's feet beating on stone floors and angry shouts mingled with jeering and laughter. When I could lie in my bed no longer, I threw on shorts and a T-shirt in the darkness and grabbed trainers as a safe option for dirty feet. I made a note to keep my back to the walls and wield my torch as a weapon, if threatened. My mind played tricks as I imagined the older boys jumping on my back and attacking me. My mouth had dried, and I longed for a bottle of water. Then, I scolded myself. Was I losing all sense of reality? But whatever the truth, my hands were damp, and I shook with fear.

The screams lead me to a tableau of horror no one should ever witness. I knew immediate action was required but honestly have no idea what I did. Did I shout first or lunge with my torch to hit the offender on the head? I'm not sure, but I sprang into action like a demented woman.

A small deaf boy called Julian, who I had photographed that day discovering the joy of coloured balloons, was now naked and tied to a bed. His hands were secured by thin rope and attached to the painted metal bars of a bedhead. His skinny legs reached halfway down the mattress and were held by two older boys who were twisting his feet at an awkward angle to gain purchase. His screams were heart-wrenching, his hair soaked in sweat and in my torch beam I could see blue eyes wide with terror. He'd wet himself.

All my fear dispersed as adrenaline flushed my body and anger rose. Somehow, I found strength and toppled the trouse-less perpetrator on to the floor, much to the amusement of the other kids. I shouted for the child to be untied, my arms whirled like windmills. Strangely, my lack of Romanian vocabulary was no handicap. The boy was released and scarpered into the darkness but not before I saw blood running down his legs.

I shouted at the boys, more for my own satisfaction than theirs. I berated them in English which must have sounded gobbledegook, but my tone could not be ignored. The thug pulled up his trousers and sloped off, grinning. As I stood in the darkness with my back to a stone wall, I internalised the enormity of the scene, but I knew nothing more could be achieved that night.

I returned to my room suffering from shock and it took over an hour for my hands to stop shaking. My vulnerability was suddenly very real in a camine that was drenched in systematic brutality. It sickened me to the core of my being.

There was no sleep. I wedged the heavy sewing-machine table under the door handle in my room and waited, hour by hour until the pale, grey light turned to rose and gold. A new day emerged but the old one would never be erased from my mind.

After that horrifying night I realised little Julian had no one to fight his corner. He didn't appear at breakfast, so I asked one of the older girls to help in the search while I beat a path to the director's office.

I hounded her the minute she arrived for work and found it hard to contain my fury. How could she not know what was happening in her camine? Why was there no one on duty at night to prevent such behaviour? So many questions filled my head and my usually moderated temper threatened to boil over.

I was invited into the inner sanctum of the office. Coffee was ordered although I was not in the mood for socialising. The director and I used limited French vocabulary while I struggled to make my case. It was perfectly clear she knew what I was trying to tell her – sign language for what I had witnessed, is much the same in any language. She shrugged her shoulders, uninterested, and carried on with her paperwork. I was dumbstruck - this was a fast-learning curve for me. I now knew those kids had no allies. This atrocity was being passed off as 'normal behaviour.'

Eventually I managed to find Julian hiding in the pigpen. I tempted him out with a sweet and gently checked to see if he was still bleeding. He was happy to be found and allowed me to brush the straw from his little body. He needed a cuddle although there was a distinct aroma of pig about him. I took him to the kitchen and asked cook for a cup of milk. Julian sat on my lap and drank it before being tempted to join some younger boys who were playing with a coloured ball, I'd given them. The next day Julian disappeared. A permanent move to another camine was arranged within twenty-four hours and I never saw him again. Harsh realities were coming thick and fast.

With hindsight, that experience was instrumental in strengthening my determination to make a difference, however small, in that decaying land. It was probably what kept me coming back over the years and it was certainly the defining moment that stopped me ever giving up, even when the quest to make a difference shrank from my line of vision. What I could not have known, back then, was that three of those teenage, bullying boys would become part of my extended family. I'd grow to love them in a way that would surprise not only me, but my family and friends, too. Those boys were caught in a sickening life cycle of violence and self-preservation. I could forgive them their appalling behaviour because they knew no better.

'I never cared when the women hit me. I laughed at them, even when they used a broom.'

Dorin – a survivor of the camine in Giurcani

Very soon after my arrival I prepared a work regime as I knew routine would help with the enormity of the task. I chose to concentrate on one room that called to me more than any other. This salon consisted of eight children who neither spoke nor responded to the human voice; they made no effort to acknowledge my existence. So, I stood in that dark, soulless room and told them this was a turning point in their lives. I would make a difference, I told them. It was of no consequence to them, and I felt less confident than my words suggested.

I was not alone in the camine for long. People came from Holland, England and France to help and we felt we had safety in numbers. There was a rush of enthusiasm to begin making changes. Gradually, everyone acclimatised to the stench of communal living and the nauseous reek of human deprivation. Eventually, if we stayed long enough, we learned to turn a blind eye to the piles and puddles of various hues and textures lingering on the floors as sometimes they defied even the most persistent mop and bucket. But what I never quite mastered was how to rinse the stark images of those thin legs, the blackened teeth and chocolate eyes. Yes, it was the eyes, mostly, that haunted my dreams.

An English volunteer called Angela came via Jane Clarke at Marks and Spencer Norwich and together we devised a programme that we hoped would achieve results in the three months we had at our disposal. It wasn't easy. We set up a daily feeding and washing programme for the children confined to cots and tried to introduce basic play and stimulation. When I looked at the children in my chosen room, I was unsure if many would live to see any results. Some did not.

Angela was younger than me but equally as committed to making a difference for those children. We talked a lot about our hopes for the work we intended to do and debated how the staff might come to accept us. I had paediatric nurse training to fall back on, but Angela had a commercial background and was full of concerns about her ability to cope. She feared not being strong enough to tackle the task. I privately thought she'd cope better than me. I could feel a range of emotions inside me that I thought were tucked into deep pockets, long ago. I was fearful to put my hand in to examine them again. Unwanted children - that was rather too close for comfort. As an illegitimate child who'd known both the fostering, adoption and care system, I was suddenly fearful about managing the emotional aspects at the camine. I knew the daily, hands-on routine would be second nature to me, but other things plagued my mind.

Over the next few weeks, Angela and I supported one another and found strength from working together. Other volunteers came and went so it was mostly us against the world when we tried to make changes. We had discovered a time-warp where seventy children were squeezed by the prejudice of communism until they gasped and choked on the corruption of those in power.

Was I arrogant to think I could achieve anything in that alien world? How could I make a difference to the camine system, the horrors of which were endemic throughout the land? Misery was ingrained in walls and children were dying. In my opinion, those who slipped away quietly were the lucky ones. But if I had a degree of arrogance, I have forgiven myself and renamed it 'get-up-and-go'. No one from a civilised country could have anticipated the reality.

It was obvious to all volunteers that the Romanian government needed to change, as did the Romanian people's attitudes to disability. But that was clearly not going to happen any time soon. Not only was money needed, but the desire to change needed to precede it. Somehow, it had a familiar ring about our own not-so-perfect country, too.

As the weeks slid by, I noticed the young people in the village all longed to go to Britain. They believed our streets were paved with gold; our land was their Utopia. But to me, they were unsophisticated kids who were likely to sink without trace in our society. Over the weeks I witnessed the close family bonds and the simplicity of their lives. There was much to admire. However, I could not imagine them in our towns and cities. Little did I know, one day in the not-too-distant future, they would be living amongst us.

The children in my salon needed weaning off the bottles of milk which were thrown into their cots twice a day and persuaded to take solid food. They were so weak and fragile it seemed a monumental task and I was almost afraid to touch them for fear they might break. But they were already broken.

Angela's children in her salon were a little more able, but still in need of better food and exercise. Most of all, these children needed human contact and love and we were desperate to take them outside for fresh air and play. We needed to wash them and somehow persuade the women to keep them clean, but to achieve that we needed soap and clean clothes daily. This involved another fight with the director who hoarded all donated items as if World War Three was on the horizon. I found everything an uphill struggle and realised the enormity of the task I'd taken on.

Angela and I became heartily sick of our miserable room in the camine and always felt sleep deprived and grubby. I missed living with the Ursu family. However, after a few weeks of living hell the friendly deputy director, Lena, came to our rescue. She found us in the salons one afternoon and told us she had a neighbour who may be able to help improve our living conditions. She suggested Angela and I visit a village lady called Maria who might have a spare couple of rooms we would rent.

I think we probably went immediately to find the said Maria. We couldn't bear to wait until the end of the day. I remember Dorin tagged along, assuring us he knew where Maria lived. He never wanted to miss an event and as we walked, he told us the entire life story of Maria, or so we guessed. He suggested she was *'tock-tock'*, which we took to mean a little on the loony side!

Maria's house was a five-minute walk from the camine on one of the dirt-track lanes and we found the lady of the house working in her garden. She was duly informed who we were by Dorin and the gate, which was bolted securely, was unlocked to allow us inside. After some initial garbled discussion, of which we understood little, she showed us the available rooms. Maria was a strident woman who never grasped our difficulty with her language.

We were offered interconnecting rooms, and each had a single bed and bedside table. A small stove to warm food and boil water was an unexpected extra in one of the rooms. The accommodation was clean, with rugs on the floor and a vast array of religious pictures all over the walls. It seemed Maria was a keen collector of dolls although we were later told they belonged to her daughter who had moved away when she got married.

We were delighted with Maria's offer and agreed to move in that day. I can't remember how we came to agree the rent, but it was somehow settled, and we paid one week in advance. It was a pittance. Something in the region of ten pounds each for a month.

There were no washing facilities at our new home, but we utilised rainwater collected in buckets each time there was a shower. I can remember on one occasion standing under a leaking gutter during a ferocious rainstorm and thinking all my birthdays had come at once. I washed my hair and body in exquisite running water and how precious was that commodity during the hot summer. We were given access to the family 'hole in the ground' lavatory and discovered one was much the same as another; none of the village loos had anything to recommend them.

Maria's husband Nicu was a quiet, insignificant man whenever Maria was around. However, when she was elsewhere, he was a lovely, gentle man who took delight in having foreign visitors in his home. He often gave us produce from his vegetable patch and on many occasions, he sat with us in amicable silence as we enjoyed the evening sun.

I particularly enjoyed Maria's pretty garden which was a blaze of colour; it was full to bursting with flowers of every variety. Fountains of pink and white, mauves and yellows met the eye from our windows and the evening fragrance from the stocks and roses was especially welcome after a day of hard work in the camine.

We were grateful to be living there, although our landlady was a strange old bird. She was given to complaining about her hard life, often demonstrating the areas of her body which were affected by pain. She never grasped that we couldn't understand much of what she said, however, as long as we made sympathetic noises in the right places, she was happy.

Maria often came into our rooms uninvited and plonked her large frame on a bed. She wore a peasant dress of rough, brown cloth, a headscarf of indistinct colour and plastic sandals. She always looked grubby, but standards of hygiene weren't high on the priority list of villagers. For many, mere existence was almost beyond reach. Maria's poor hands were calloused and grimed with dirt and were, she informed us, full of arthritis. Her ankles were permanently swollen and there was often a distinct odour around her.

One day Maria asked how old we were and we both drew our ages in the dirt. When I asked her own age, we were shocked to find she was only five years older than me. A large part of her life had been under dictatorship and no one will ever fully know the extent of hardship Ceausescu inflicted on his people. Maria died in 2002.

Angela and I devised a washing routine whereby we used rain or well water and doused the flowers with the leftovers. Our clothes were washed in an old enamel bowl with the equivalent of Sunlight soap. The hard bars of waxy soap produced very little lather but were the only product we could find when our initial supply was used up. We hung our smalls on the line and marvelled at how quickly everything dried in the Romanian sunshine.

Maria and her husband kept chickens and geese which wandered around the garden. Chicken wire fences were common in all gardens in Romanian villages and Maria's was no exception. But somehow the chicks always managed to escape, and she was forever hunting for them, often not in a good mood. We thought she held us responsible for anything that went missing and she often took our non-communication in her language as a personal affront.

Maria's attempt to increase the rent was an almost weekly occurrence. I witnessed more than one ding-dong battle between Maria and Angela. Nicu and I used to sit and raise eyebrows in amazement at the ability of two women to fight without a common language between them. We never increased the rent, well, not during that visit. In subsequent years when I travelled alone, Maria used to blackmail me into giving her more money and I used to justify my soft-heartedness on the basis that life was tough for her, as it was for all villagers and it really wasn't much money to me.

Dorin, Gheorgie and Adrian were regular visitors to our new home. They loved the garden and told us the names of the flowers and trees. Initially, Maria was not keen to have camine kids on her land, but she eventually came to like them. And it was thanks to the many visits by the boys that Angela and I picked up the Romanian language so quickly. They never stopped talking. They were fascinated by our attempts to speak their language and our 'foreign ways'. We both had a lot of fun with them in the evenings after work and those times are some of my happiest memories. Our daily chores at the camine became easier in the knowledge we had somewhere clean and private to go home to.

I became aware that the time and effort given by the few skilled volunteers who stayed for more than a week or so, would take years to impact on the deprivation. The plight of Romania's children was country wide and urgent. No one found answers and the situation was dire beyond belief. Most volunteers returned home full of disillusionment where there had been an abundance of hope. For me, the barriers I met only strengthened my determination to make a difference.

Chapter 4

'I liked looking after the pigs. I used to hide in the outbuildings and cuddle the babies when they were born. It felt safe there.'

Dorin – a survivor of the camine in Giurcani

Adrian

I don't remember when Rita first arrived in our village. I can remember lots of things arriving like clothes and toys, so I guess it was around then when she first came to visit. We had loads of English people come to the village over the years. They all brought us stuff but none of them stayed for long. Only Rita kept coming back.

I don't really like women much. They always want me to do something and scream at me and call me stupid. But not Rita. I'd do anything to make her pleased with me. I used to dream that she was my mother when I was younger, but I don't dream that anymore. She's the best thing that ever happened to me.

Rita and Angela liked me. Most of the others liked the little kids better. Rita used to play games and teach me songs in English, and I used to sing Romanian folk songs I'd learned by hanging around village weddings. Rita said I had a voice like an angel but I don't know what angels sound like so I can't say whether it was true or not. She was always saying, 'Sing, Adrian, sing'. I always want to please her, so I'd sing any time she asked.

41

The first time she came, when I was just a kid, she hung around with us older boys a lot. For the first year or so she visited with Angela and then after that she started coming on her own. One year I was told she'd got married and I remember being worried in case her new husband didn't like us and stopped her coming to Romania. But lucky for us that didn't happen. Eric likes us and we like him too.

I was afraid of the staff at the camine. They beat me so often for not doing what they asked even though I tried my best. I'm what people call 'slow'. I don't always understand what people want and I don't remember things, either. I have fits sometimes. I'm supposed to have tablets but the camine often ran out of them and I didn't have any for months. My fits got worse and then I had to have the doctor to look at me. When the doctor came to check me, the director used to say she had run out of my tablets. One of the women told me they were sold to people in the village, but I don't know if that's true.

Dorin

I once heard someone say, 'If God wanted us to travel at the speed of light, he'd have stuck a jet-propelled motor up our asses!' I suppose if He'd wanted me to have parents or proper legs, He'd have sorted that, too. But He didn't, and I was dumped in the camine as a kid and stayed for a good chunk of my life as a grown-up, too. Not that I'm moaning about it. I learnt at a young age that you have to get on with what life throws at you and hope it gets better.

Back when I was young, I just wanted enough food to eat and some shoes that would fit my cranky feet. Well, they're not feet, really. Just stumps. Rita says my deformities remind her of some kids born in England years ago. Apparently, it was to do with a drug the mothers took that caused babies to be born without arms and legs. I don't know what my mother took, or if she took anything at all, but I've got no proper hands or feet. I have a single finger on each arm that sticks out from where my elbow should be. But they work just fine. My legs are short, too, with twisted lumps of flesh where other people have feet. Some people call me a midget, but I'm not. I've seen midgets on television, and they have funny faces. But I'm good-looking. I've got dark brown eyes that Rita tells me have a twinkle, and I've got good hair and good teeth as well. I think that kind of balances out the bad bits, don't you? The first time I saw a photo of my face (I can't remember when it was, but I was grown-up) I remember thinking, 'I'm quite a handsome man!' And then I remembered my hands and feet.

At some point I realised my dream of having a wife and settling down with a couple of kids was never going to happen. But that's life and it's no use hankering after things you can't have, is it? There was a girl in the village I liked when I was younger. She told me I had beautiful brown eyes and I thought that meant she fancied me. But she didn't. When I asked if she'd like to go for a walk to the river, she screamed at me. 'With a freak like you?' she bellowed, so that half the village heard. I wanted to die of embarrassment. The village men teased me about it for years. I've never dared ask a girl to go anywhere with me since. And now that girl is married with three kids. And guess what? She's not pretty anymore – but I'm still good looking.

Nothing stops me doing anything I want except I can't walk in deep snow. I sink - just like a cartoon character I've watched on television. I find myself up to my neck in frozen ice and I have to be rescued. When I was a kid, I couldn't go outside in the winter in case I got lost in a snowdrift.

Rita told me, years ago, that I could achieve anything if I really set my heart on it. I thought to myself that day, I'll have a house of my own in the village, please. I didn't tell her, but it set me dreaming about what could be possible.

43

Life in the camine wasn't as bad as you might think. I had good mates, Adrian, Gheorgie and Dan, and we did have a laugh sometimes. And at least we could go outside the camine building and into the village, unlike most of the kids who were tied to their beds or locked in dark, stinking rooms. So that was lucky, for a start. But we had to work hard, all day long and often again after supper in the summer months. And that was tough for kids, especially without enough to eat. Someone told me that your body adapts to having too little food and you still manage to work. Well, I'm living proof, aren't I?

It was not long after the Romanian people shot Ceausescu that I learnt how lucky I really was. And it wasn't 'cos the dictator was dead either. He never bothered me when he was alive, so I wasn't bothered when they shot him. No – being lucky started one hot, sunny day, years and years ago. It was when Rita appeared in the village to work at the camine and I found out she really liked me. She was the first person who ever liked me. I didn't know it at the time, but she was going to change my life forever.

I know it was summer when she came 'cos the crops were high in the fields and flies were hugging the cow dung - you know the ones that always look like they're having a feast and can't get enough shit in their greedy mouths. (See – there's always someone with a worse life than you!) This particular lucky day, I remember, was a day when the flies were being a menace and if you weren't careful, they'd give you a nasty bite. The dust from the land caught on the breeze and managed to get in your eyes and mouth as if it owned you. It was the time of day when the camine staff sat outside to take a rest from the hard work in the kid's rooms. They had a bucket of water and dipped a metal cup in and passed it around the group. Sometimes they'd offer us kids a drink, but I don't think they did that day.

They were laughing at Rita and Angela because they'd started doing stuff in the little kids' salons that nobody had ever done before. They tried to clean their filthy asses and feed them proper food. I was worried if the little kids had too much, there'd be less for me. I don't know how she did it, but Rita persuaded the director to let her bring the kids outside to get some fresh air. Most of the kids were sitting on rugs on the concrete pathway and they'd been given bowls of water to play with. Some kids had to be propped up on the wall 'cos they couldn't sit properly, and the sun made them all squint.

The camine women were bitching about the English. They thought Rita should know better than to wear shorts at her age. I must admit, the English women were dressed in funny clothes and they jabbered to each other in some queer language none of us understood, but I thought they looked nice. Both of them looked fresh and clean and kind and I was curious to know more about them. They definitely came from a country that was better than ours. They probably had lives like king's wives with servants to bring them everything they needed, I thought.

Bogdan, the groundsman looked at them full of hate. Or was it envy? He hated everybody and that included us kids. 'Why would those stupid women want to waste money and energy on mad kids?' he wanted to know, flapping his hand to find some breeze. 'You're all crazy.' He glared straight at me like I was mud under his shoe. 'You kids are a waste of space.' He was smoking a thin rollup which he'd lit from a match he struck on the sole of his shoe. I remember he coughed, he always coughed and then he sniffed loudly and spat brown gunge into the dust. 'Pity Ceausescu didn't do away with you and have done with it', he muttered to no one in particular, but I knew he meant me.

Now, I was never afraid of anything, until then. But I felt goosebumps prickle my arms that day and a real fear crept into my head. I've never forgotten it. Even though it was a hot day, I went cold just thinking about what he'd said. I'd never liked Bogdan 'cos he'd given me too many beatings, but after I realised how much he hated us kids I knew he was a real threat. I could be smothered while I slept or taken away and drowned like a puppy. I'd seen kittens and puppies drowned in the river, loads of times. No one would know what happened to me and no one would have cared, either. But years have gone by and he's dead, which is what he deserved, and I'm still here. Ha!

I remember that day for two reasons. Not just because I learnt to fear Bogdan, but because it turned out to be the start of a new life for me. The two foreign women who'd arrived in our village started the changes to my life, although it was several years before the really good bit happened. I've got a memory that one of them smelled of flowers and the other had red hair tied back in a ribbon. They were both taller than me (most people are taller than me.) But they were even taller than Adrian.

Gheorgie

I don't know much but I know I like the English, 'specially Rita 'cos she always comes back. I loved Angela too. She made me laugh. None of the others come back but Rita told me they all have busy lives and lots to do, so I suppose I understand.

I don't remember where I was before I came to Giurcani. And I don't talk as much or ask questions like other kids. I listen a lot.

I wouldn't like to live in a town because they don't have animals there. I think I like sheep the best. When they're little they're soft and I like cuddling them. They smell nice too.

Umm…..I've been treated badly you know. A lot when I was young. I never think I've done anything wrong, but I must have or they wouldn't have beaten me. Sometimes they take our food away as punishment. They shouldn't do that should they? Everyone needs to eat. I think I could be fatter.

Chapter 5

'When I first saw my face in a mirror, I discovered I'm handsome. How can anyone not know what they look like until they're a man?'

Gheorgie – a survivor of the camine in Giurcani

I learnt that when well-meaning people from wealthy countries start a crusade to 'rescue' human beings, they should swallow a huge dose of reality before setting out. Everyone should examine their motives. Before travelling to Romania, I should have made the effort to understand the people I wanted to help, considered their beliefs and the historical facts and customs of the country. And maybe I should have asked myself two burning questions, 'why am I doing this and what is the likelihood of success?' Nothing is worse than failure where human lives are concerned. And heaven knows, I faced that prospect often enough. Of course, the flip side of that argument is, if I'd known what was ahead of me when I left England, I doubt I would have lifted my feet from home soil. I tried not to beat myself up too much about what I couldn't achieve, and as the weeks turned into months, we just got on with the job in the best way possible.

I learned human suffering is not only traumatic to work amongst, but once the project is embarked upon, you have a responsibility to do your best, achieve positive results and above all, to ensure you do no harm. It didn't take rocket science to see Romania should be helped to look after her own children, but the issue was how best to achieve it. I hated to see Romanian children adopted into homes outside of their own country, but I learned to keep that view to myself. Many adopted children were deported into European homes and research tells us that some placements were successful. Some were not. I felt Romania needed to crawl out of her slum of despair and forge a new life, but progress was fraught with difficulties. A concerted effort was needed from the Romanian government, neighbouring countries and most of all, the Romanian people themselves. But at Giurcani, there was only me.

One of the big questions I asked myself was – if volunteers succeeded in changing the camine regime, what infra-structure was in place to support the changes? And specifically, where would those camine children live if someone closed the only home they'd known? I knew there were hundreds, if not thousands of camines all over Romania where children were hidden away like dirty little secrets.

I developed a special friendship with a couple of similar age to me who lived at the far end of the village. Didi Rotaru, the schoolteacher, and his charming wife Tori were to become lifelong friends and their home a sanctuary on many occasions. Didi gave me history lessons about the plight of his country as my Romanian language skills advanced, and I imagine I sat with open mouth as the atrocities of communism were revealed. And I came to realised it was not realistic to think

Romanian lives could be brought into line with western civilisation. A huge rethink was needed if I was to endure my time in his country.

In 1991 and for the years to come, I made mistakes. I blush when I remember some of them. I learnt that foreign aid must both educate and encourage recipients to be pro-active. People living in poverty need to engage with the process of change if it is to be meaningful. Piling material stuff into villages is not the answer. People have pride - even poor people have their pride. Too often, I've watched foreigners create mayhem when they've arrived with lorries full of aid; I've seen chaos disrupt communities despite the best of intentions. Material goods have been fought over and stolen and consequently, disharmony has washed through villages. I've learnt that giving material possessions is never enough and it doesn't take long for generosity to be taken for granted.

At the other end of the scale, on my initial visit I met a scary lady who, in the name of 'Christianity', intended to move into the village of Giurcani and 'run it'. That can't be done, either. People must run their own lives. Luckily, that lady, and her ideals soon disappeared. As for me, I'm still trying to get it right after twenty-nine years.

I discovered that the village of Giurcani sits within one of the poorest regions of Romania. Its need was palpable. A fault line of communities nestled around Giurcani and all were desiccated by Ceausescu and his regime. Romanian people were growing old before their time, burdened and bent from bearing too many children and the excruciating, physical work.

Contaminated water and disease were causing illness and premature mortality. Lack of money and opportunity had also taken its toll over four decades. I met dozens of people born into communism and for them, the death of Ceausescu presented as many questions as answers.

I visited tumble-down houses with leaking straw roofs and damp, earthen floors. The fireplaces had long gone cold from lack of firewood. One mug, a plate and fork were often their only possessions. I found it hard to believe that people from Europe were living in such isolation and squalor. I had always associated abject poverty with third world countries.

I knew little about the politics of the country beyond the fact that the people shot their dictator on Christmas Day in 1989. But as I got to grips with the language, villagers told me their stories. Family treasures looted by soldiers. Humiliating 'examinations' if women failed to produce a child every year, and so much more. And the new regime was no better than the old one, they told me. Many of the deposed communist leaders were reputedly still in power and for them, life was easy. Everyone knows money and power corrupt in any society on earth and for the wealthy people of Romania, there were no problems. But the majority of people were hungry, particularly in the cities; jobs were hard to find and the people were frightened. By the second Christmas after his death many wished the dictator had never been shot.

Romania is a vast, beautiful country hampered by historical, grinding deprivation and blinkered people in power. As a country, she is judged harshly by many for her documented 'orphanage sins' and her felons and criminals who tip-up in our country. But the people I met were warm and friendly and offered hospitality, even when they had little for themselves.

Travellers to the eastern edge of Europe can enjoy everything from bustling cities to quiet backwaters and may be surprised by the vastness of the terrain. Swathes of the country are breathtakingly beautiful. It is true, Romania is a little rough around the edges, particularly if we judge her by the standard of her hotels and restaurants. However, from the soft folds of her pastureland, the swell of the mighty Danube to the monasteries of the Carpathian Mountains, she is my kind of country. Her organic countryside blazes with wildflowers in springtime and the mouths of Romania's rivers yield a banquet to visiting birds amid their wetlands and marshes. In summer, a roaring heat singes flowers and foliage to a crisp and creates a palette of gold and burnt sienna across the land. My favourite season in Giurcani was always the winter when drifting snow softened the frayed edges of heartlands and forests into an undulating, giant pillow. However, in the cities mounds of white grubbiness piled high against crumbled buildings and slush and snow halted footsteps and chilled bones. The snow resisted all efforts with brush and shovel and winters followed a relentless pattern. Snow will surely fall again tomorrow.

Juxtaposed around the camines, I discovered Romania's towns and cities concealed stunning architecture, albeit a little jaded. Grand, intricate buildings had been created from her former wealth by clever, educated people. During the nineteen-twenties and thirties, Bucharest was known as 'little Paris' and entertained royalty alongside the wealthiest of the world's society. Ornate, gilded opera houses exist in comparatively small towns and bear witness to a glorious past.

But not so glorious, of course, her more recent history where millstones of neglect were hung around little necks. This is a country anxious to snip loose the label of the 'orphanage scandal', but I suspect it will be many decades before she'll be rewarded. To date, Romania has not fully cleaned up her act and I believe it will take several generations and a dogged desire to forge lasting change. But I note and hang on every small improvement, otherwise I would never go back, would I?

As the last century flipped a page, Romania continued to drag the baggage of communism behind her. Experience had taught her many negatives, particularly to accept what couldn't be changed. But the metal fences and hording of material possessions will linger long, for who knows when another dictator could make their lives a living hell?

I developed a strange fascination with a junk yard of old tractors and machinery not far from Giurcani. For me it became symbolic of Romanian life under democracy. Over the years I had photographed ever growing heaps of rusty, twisted metal as they grew skyward and I asked Didi Rotaru about the expanding heap of machinery. He told me that after the fall of communism, there was no longer money to repair anything. No spare parts were available due to the closure of manufacturing plants and loss of jobs. The poverty trap had tightened its grip and they were hard facts for me to grasp. Surely, nothing can be worse than communism, can it?

Over the next decade I saw the once flourishing co-operative farms diminish at a staggering rate. There had been hundreds of acres of food grown on government-owned farms around Giurcani, all harvested by communal machinery. Now that land is dug by hand. Fields of corn have become a thing of the past. Herds of cattle disappeared and that in turn affected the milk yield; this of course, impacted on cheese and butter production. Few calves were born which made the cost of buying a family cow prohibitive for most families. It was unimaginable how life could get any worse for those families.

Chapter 6

'The volunteers told me I have 'special needs' but I grew up being told I was mad. I'm happy I'm not mad.'

Adrian – survivor of the camine in Giurcani

Dorin

I shall never forget the night the Romanian people shot Ceausescu. But I should go back a week or so before it happened and tell you how it began. I know all about it because I'm a good listener. If the women gossiped when they should be working, they often didn't notice if I hung around. I sometimes think that because I've got no hands and feet people think I have no brain, either. But I remember things and I'm not afraid to say what I think about life.

I know the trouble started in Timisoara. There was a priest there who spoke out about Ceausescu's bad ways. He complained about him not feeding the people. And then soldiers came to arrest the priest for saying those things. The people tried to protect the priest but there were scuffles in the town. The trouble spread and there was another lot of trouble in Iasi which is only two hours away from Giurcani. I heard that the soldiers soon stamped on that and men were sent to prison.

A worker at the camine had a small radio that he used to listen to when he was working. I often sat with him in his hut if I was hiding from the director. I heard the speeches Ceausescu

54

made about telling us that life would soon get better. People told me he built himself a huge palace in Bucharest with more rooms than he could use, while the rest of us were hungry. His palace had more than a thousand rooms and some were as big as a football field, I was told. What sort of man does that? But we had to be careful what we said because you never knew who was listening. Not that I cared much. What could anybody do to me? I was already stuck in a prison for kids with not enough to eat and had a good beating most days.

When the 'big happening' started it was very cold with snow everywhere and it was late at night. Violetta, who was married to Sandel, ran up to the camine with a story that Ceausescu had run away and the people were angry. They were out looking for him, she said. I knew it couldn't be true because no one would dare to chase our leader. Ceausescu was like a god to the people, and everyone did what he said, no matter how bad life was. Sandel told Violetta to go back home to their kids and not talk such rubbish, but she told him he would see that she was right in the morning. After she had gone Sandel turned on his radio and we sat and listened in amazement.

After the trouble around the towns, Ceausescu talked on TV to the people to say there were some 'hooligans' around who were saying bad things about him. No one was to take any notice of them, he said. He promised he was going to give the people more pensions and good wages and that things were going to get better. But the crowd weren't listening to him. We could hear on the radio they were booing and jeering him and that they were getting angry. I couldn't believe how they dared to do that. Everyone listened to him, always. When the crowd became so angry that they were dangerous, the army sent an aeroplane that looked like a big bird into the palace. It swooped down and picked up our leader and his wife and flew away with them. His three children were not there.

The next day was like no other day in my life. This is what it was like. When the women came to work, they huddled in groups talking about the news. The director told them to get on with their work, but the minute she went back to the office they started talking again. They heard on the news that when the big bird aeroplane dropped Ceausescu and his wife on the ground the army picked them up in a tank and took them to safety. People told me you could see it on television. Everyone was so angry that they stormed the place where he was, dragged him and his wife outside and shot them dead.

Well, no one could believe it. There was singing and dancing in the village for two days. Everyone was drinking and saying that life would now get better. 'Good riddance to Ceausescu!' they shouted. I was glad he was dead. No one felt sorry for him, but no one had any idea what to expect from life in the future either. Who would be put in charge? Who would be our leader?

Adrian.

At first, I thought Rita was the new leader of our village. I think that's what the women told me – she was sent by the government to keep order and report back. But she smiled too much and seemed to like us, so I knew that couldn't be true. She didn't speak any words I could understand, and I noticed the village people were wary of all the foreigners. But back then, everyone was wary of strangers. You never knew what trouble they could cause. Under Ceausescu they weren't allowed to have foreigners in their homes or even speak to them. No wonder we were a bit afraid of Rita and Angela.

I soon learnt all the foreign people visiting the village were called 'volunteers'. That seemed to mean they gave us things and were kind to us. Lots of them visited that year. They came from France, Holland, Ireland and Germany, places I'd never heard of. But one of those foreigners from England had something in her eyes that said she would never let anyone harm me again. I knew she really liked me and I knew I could trust her. I'd never trusted anyone before.

Gheorgie

I'm a quiet sort of chap and I can't stand it when people shout at me. It gives me a headache. At the camine I was given the grotty things to do like shovelling shit out of beds and cleaning floors. I used to work in the laundry and that was hard; washing for seventy children even when most of us had little to wear, it was still a big job.

One day the director told me she had a special job for me and Viorel and we had to stay inside and wait for her to call us. Quite soon a huge lorry came up the driveway and when men opened it we saw it was full to the top with clothes. We had a special room in the camine where spare clothes were kept, and it was always locked. The director opened it up for us to carry everything inside. There were foreign people in the lorry who smiled a lot and seemed to like me. One of them put a blue and yellow cap on my head, so I gave him a hug.

After Viorel and me had helped get all the clothes from the lorry into the building the director took the foreigners into the office and made them coffee. I still had the cap and was hoping I could keep it. I'd never had a cap before. Much later the lorry left and we all waved goodbye; I was sad they went 'cos they were kind to me. As soon as the lorry was on the bottom road the director snatched the cap off my head, hit me around the ears and said, 'idiots can't have a cap.' I wasn't surprised, but for a short while it had been mine. Two days later I saw the director's eldest son wearing it and so I forgot about it.

Chapter 7

'I can't stand the noise in this place. Kids are always screaming from hunger and they give me a headache. I often get headaches you know.'

Gheorgie - a survivor of the camine in Giurcani

It took a while to get used to the methods and routines of the camine and make plans to improve the kid's lives, even in small ways. The women were terrified of the director; and sustained lashings from her acid tongue whenever the mood took her. Each day was a struggle for them, but also for us. Our simplest requests were met with resistance and the women were bewildered by our attempt to make changes. They were afraid to comply with our requests and insisted everything must be channelled through the director. We fully understood their concerns and consulted the director about everything. I was usually voted the one to ask favours from the director as I wasn't afraid of her, although some volunteers hated to be within twenty feet of her. But her indifference made me angry which gave me courage to fight for those children, and there were many ding-dong battles between us.

Angela and I developed a growing relationship with the deputy to the camine director. Lena had a daughter training to be a social worker in Vaslui and therefore probably had some insight into our aims. Her daughter worked with distressed children and I think Lena learnt from her that it was time for change. I don't think the director misunderstood our intentions - she simply preferred the old regime which was easier than making changes. For her, changes made more work.

The six oldest boys went out to work the farmland and operate the laundry each morning. For them there was freedom from the camine building but it was offset by immensely hard work in all weathers and insufficient food to sustain them. They were slaves to the system.

No one could tell us the age of the children or anything about their backgrounds. The children knew nothing of birthdays, Christmas, their family or what the future held for them. I guess they all just lived for the day, hoping someone would remember to feed them.

Angela and I eventually deduced that these children were not 'orphans. Well, very few. These were society's cast-offs, the hidden shame of people indoctrinated by Ceausescu's criminal ethos. They'd all arrived at the gates of Giurcani by one route or another and it took many years to piece together the mysteries surrounding only a few of them. Several children died over the years and were put to rest in the churchyard next to the camine. Each time I visited Giurcani I had an update from Dorin about the number of funerals he'd attended. Sometimes it was villagers, but often the children from the camine. At the very best, one could say the children's lives were marked by others when they died.

Angela and I worked hard to build relationships with the women, hoping that if we worked alongside them with smiles and good grace, they would come to understand our aims and we would continue to pick up the Romanian language. When the women realised we weren't the enemy but relieved them of some of their workload, they became more responsive.

Gradually, the staff began to trust us. They smiled a greeting when we arrived each morning and made efforts to communicate. There was laughter at our attempts to speak their language and I believe they came to like us although, I'm sure, they thought we were bonkers! After all, why would we be working without payment? What possessed us to live in a foreign country when we belonged in a land of plenty?

Charity was an unknown word to the Romanian people who were absorbed with the effort to survive and had never heard of people worse off than themselves. (Many years later I took part in an abseil for tsunami victims. I took a photo to show the older camine boys and it led to some weird discussions. Why was Rita dangling from a church tower on a piece of rope and how did that help poor people?)

Angela and I accepted invitations into villager's homes, met their families and learnt about their previous lives under communism. Nothing we heard was good. We noticed few women wore wedding rings and they told us the gold on their fingers had been taken long ago by soldiers who regularly checked the towns and villages to ensure women were producing a child each year to meet the dictator's edict. Some of the things we heard about life under communism were too grim to repeat, but I came to see those women as strong, determined survivors. I appreciated their kindness and hospitality which filled many long summer evenings for Angela and me that year. Didi and Tori Rotaru were special people, and the seed of a wonderful friendship was planted.

Apart from working in my chosen salon, I was keen to release the children tied to beds and those with hands secured behind their backs; Angela and I wanted to start play and music therapy with them. I discussed my plans with the director who shrugged and had little to say on the matter and I was to learn why. Everything in that camine had a consequence and unwelcome shocks were coming our way almost daily. The director stood back and waited for us to fail.

We decided to release a sweet girl called Ramona who was bedbound by strips of sheeting; we also decided to untie a boy called Constantine whose hands had been secured behind his back since our arrival. The women watched us with interest as we asked for scissors to achieve our aims. The director went home early that day.

All hell let loose! Ramona rushed out of the salon and charged into a room of small children where she started battering any child within reach. Constantine whipped the scissors from my hands and proceeded to jab his face until blood ran. These children were violent self-harmers. Out language limitations and the sheer bad will from the director meant we had no idea about the psychological state of the children or why they were confined. Our bewilderment probably raised a smile of satisfaction from the director when she heard our 'new ideas' were not so good after all.

There was no counselling service or child psychologist at hand to deal with these damaged children. They were drugged daily to keep them calm, and I thought they would be better dead. With heavy hearts we had to agree, in the short term, there was no other way to cope with the children's behaviour. Life in the camine was a self-perpetuating vicious circle and we were making little inroad. I tried hard not to dwell on the things we had no hope of achieving.

All the children were hungry. There was a monthly food ration which was considerably less than was needed to keep them nourished. And that was only one of the problems. Looking back, I have no idea why I stayed, a. I could have been sailing around the beautiful Isles of Scilly with friends. But I was ever conscious that we had so little time to make a difference and much needed to be done. The immovability of the situation depressed and often overwhelmed us.

It was essential to keep on good terms with the director even though it grated on me; I knew our differences needed to be put aside if anything was to be achieved for those children. It became obvious the problem between us was a 'woman thing' as it was noticeable the lady dealt with men in a polite and more charming way. But maybe, if I'd been in her shoes, I'd have been resentful too. We were thrust upon her and her world was opened to foreign scrutiny. It couldn't have been a good experience, particularly as loss of face is an issue in Romania. We challenged her practices while her staff looked on.

To ease passage for our aims, I spent time with the director and her deputy to try to come to an agreement about the children in the two salons where Angela and

I had chosen to work. In my room they looked like two-year olds, they had bottles of milk thrown at them three times a day and nothing vaguely resembling care. The lack of nourishment was patently obvious and as they had neither the strength nor incentive to stand, my desire to teach them to walk was a distant dream. Eventually, it was agreed I could spend time in the kitchen with Natalia and set up a feeding programme and, best of all, the women had permission to help me. I would attempt to produce something resembling baby food for our two salons and we felt it was one small step forward.

Little by little Angela and I improved our Romanian words and phrases. The older kids soon grasped the game of naming objects for us and our pronunciation caused much hilarity. We reciprocated by naming objects in English and teaching them nursery rhymes and children's songs. They were surprisingly quick to learn and were also learning to have fun for the first time in their lives. Their rendition of 'Row, row, row the boat', was something to cherish.

My room of children was a typical cramped salon with rusty cots, little light and no fresh air. When I first learned from one of the women that 'my children' were seven or eight years old, I remember my disbelief and a lot of finger counting that went on to establish the true facts. The children were wearing Marks and Spencer clothes aged two-three years and I was shocked. Of course, when I thought about it further, I realised they all had full sets of second teeth. In a way, they were quite scary, they were small and frail with large black teeth in big heads.

I started work by drawing a picture of a bottle of milk and placed it above each cot. I marked a large X through the bottle to imply no milk in a bottle should be given to this child. I discovered the Romanian word for bottle is 'sticla' so in felt pen I wrote *'no sticla'* on the notice.

I ventured into the kitchen and smiled at jolly Natalie who was the camine cook. Her smile was open and after some communication by hand gestures and some rummaging in cupboards, I was delighted to find an old-fashioned metal mouli-mincer among her utensils. I asked if I could sieve the vegetable soup that I'd spotted warming in two large saucepans on a spitting black hob. This was the children's main meal of the day, and the same as yesterday and the day before. As Natalia continued to smile, I took advantage of her good nature and proceeded to sieve some of her soup into dented metal bowls to feed the children in my room. I added stale bread for good measure. Angela wanted to join the experiment for some of her kids too. The sieving created a thickened, baby-food mixture and looked perfect.

I returned to the salon with my bounty, full of expectation that the kids would be delighted with the new concoction. Wrong! I propped the weak little scraps upon pillows, wedged them into the corner of the cots and told them they were in for a treat. As some were unable to support their own body weight, they frequently toppled over which caused distress to both them and me, so I asked for Angela's help and together we started the process of feeding the children with their first taste of solid food.

It was surreal. We were spat at and scratched while harsh screams rang down the corridors. Those frail, yet obstinate children objected to baby food being pushed into their mouths. Of course, they did. Where they mustered strength from, I had no idea and why had I not expected this response? I was carried away by my joy at making progress and never took stock of the obvious.

The clash of spoons on teeth was nerve-jingling and the spitting a little worrying with all the news about AIDS and TB. Angela held their little arms under a sheet to aid the process while I tried to sooth them with lullabies and songs. With perseverance over a number of days, they gradually took the food and I rewarded them after every meal with milk from a plastic beaker. We repeated the process with Angela's children, too.

We wanted to get the children cleaned and smelling better and found bowls and buckets in a store cupboard. We collected well water in huge plastic containers which was icy cold, but there was no chance of warming it. I successfully enticed the director to give us clothes from her store to improve the children's overall well-being.

Much to the astonishment of the staff, Angela and I worked from eight o'clock in the morning, which was breakfast time for the kids, until after the children had supper around six. We were determined to supervise all their meals. Even on Sundays we visited the children as there was absolutely nothing else to do in the village. Little by little the feeding regime of our two salons improved. If I had any idea it was the start of a new life for some of those little ones, I would have been heartily encouraged. I dared to dream that one day, Livio,

Petico and the others might strengthen from their new diet and eventually learn to walk. Many died.

We introduced the children to play using balloons and crayons and by singing songs. We clapped with huge enthusiasm to our own merriment and soon the idea caught on. Some mornings I was welcomed by clapping hands from the more able. To see a small child rock in time to the music was a milestone for us and we were often moved to tears by the enormity of the task. The days passed, one very much the same as another.

When I look back, I realise it was a hard, daily grind. *Doggedly determined* would probably describe us. Washing, feeding, potty-training and stimulating the children became a full-time job and the days and weeks flew by. Although the environment we worked in was unpleasant, the highlight of our day could be something as simple as a smile from a child who had previously never given us eye contact. Maybe a child would reach out arms to be picked-up. Cause for celebration indeed. Those small happenings lifted our spirits and in the evenings Angela and I shared news with each other and talked about it for hours. But they were only meagre drops of hope in a sea of devastation.

One day, about a month after our arrival, two French women arrived at the camine. They told us their remit was to oversee initial explorations for bringing water into the building from a bore hole on a distant hill. They worked for a French charity called Equi-libre and told us the plans and funding were in place and they intended to return to the camine when pipe work started. Apparently, the results of their initial drilling showed there was sufficient water underground and they planned to build bathrooms and indoor lavatories for which a sewer system would be needed. Collaboration between the French and the English resulted in rooms being set aside in the newly planned Marks and Spencer extension to accommodate the bathrooms. We were thrilled, knowing this would greatly benefit our own work, too.

Marks and Spencer sent a surveyor to the camine to arrange for the extension to get under way and we spent happy hours with Pat who was fresh from civilisation. He, of course, was shocked by what he saw.

Slowly, the extension would rise from the parched Romanian soil although it would not be started during our three months at the camine. But the reality of it was like food for the soul. It would afford less crowded sleeping arrangements and ways to keep the children clean.

A massive amount of work was undertaken by the French team and at great expense. Indoor plumbing appeared over the next year, sparkling washbasins and showers were installed to a standard I would welcome in my own home. Hopes were on the rise. We were told of the 'grand turning-on ceremony' when water gushed forth, much to the delight of Dorin and others who would benefit.

However, all was not as it appeared. The sad outcome was that no water ran through the pipes after the first four weeks and the brand-new bathrooms were never used again. How or why the survey was incorrect we never found out, however the water issue rumbled on for many more years to come

Chapter 8

'The English were a bit funny. They wore short trousers and smelled nice.'

Adrian – a survivor of the camine in Giurcani

In 1991, the border with Russia was a mere three miles from Giurcani; the bordering country is now known as Moldova. I remember the sense of curiosity and slight fear that Russia's proximity prompted in me. (I'd probably read too many Cold War spy stories.) I wanted to glimpse the harsh, tail-end of Europe. I thought it could break the monotony of camine life and maybe feel like a 'short break'? How that idea amuses me when I think back on my naivety. Luckily, I was assured by villagers that I would find nothing but beggars and thieves and, although I could cross the border into Russia with ease, I would not be allowed back into Romania.

The military presence on the border confirmed the advice and the weapon-wielding soldiers suggested it would not be prudent to try. It certainly put another slant on life and my curiosity waned overnight. Lost in Russia was one step too far, even for me. I did, from time to time, see small groups of men who were said to have slipped over the border into Romania at night. They carried an array of trashy trinkets to sell or barter with destitute villagers. I was assured that life in parts of Russia was worse than the poverty in Romania. This was hard to grasp, living as I was among such hardship and deprivation. There was an incongruity about people wanting to escape *to* Romania when we all wanted to alleviate Romania's suffering. Had we got it wrong? I asked myself more than once.

Hospitality in the village could be anything from a beer to a meat-laden meal and not all of it was pleasurable. But the kindness shown to me was beyond reproach. Those families lived literally, from hand to mouth and their entire source of food was produced on their land. There was a bartering system running throughout the village which brought a little variation to their diet.

The hard work of planting and cultivating crops fell mainly to the women. Everything was done entirely with hand tools since the fall of communism, and was always weather-dependent. There was no access to pesticides and basic animal dung was used as fertiliser. The land was never replenished with minerals or phosphates and lack of summer rain could ruin the entire crop.

Animals were reared in back yards; pigs, sheep, chickens, ducks and geese lived beside the essential guard dogs which came in a myriad of shapes, colours and degrees of ferocity. Chickens were killed by the women on an ad hoc basis and went into tasty stews and soups. The killing of the pig or sheep was a huge family occasion which took place once or twice a year and was always executed by the man of the house. The animal was slaughtered by slitting its throat and it was then hung from the nearest tree. Here it would drip blood for many hours before the knife went in, to butcher it into sizable chunks. The offal was fried, flesh was roasted or minced, and the intestines used to make delicious sausages. There was always an aromatic feast for the family on the day of the slaughter, but much of the meat was either salted or frozen to provide for the coming months.

Fruit and vegetables were grown throughout the spring and summer and the women preserved them in brine or syrup in large, air-tight glass jars. Tomatoes, aubergines and courgettes were all bottled and stored for the winter in underground cellars which were cool all the year round. I remember one hot summer I arrived when the watermelon season was at its best. Huge chunks of reddish-pink flesh were served up by Tori and we slurped the juices while listening to the hum of Didi's bees in the garden. The village women made their own tomato puree and they pickled eggs, gherkins and onions. Cobs of ripened corn were stored in massive cages and used for animal fodder in the winter while some was ground into flour for cooking.

There was one shop in the village in the early years selling very little, and a trip to Birlad was difficult and costly. I only made the journey by horse and cart once. The pain of the twenty miles there and twenty miles home was never forgotten. A sore backside in Romania was too much to bear!

Self-sufficiency was vital. Even those who travelled to Birlad found nothing but jars of vegetable and tins of miserable, pallid meat to purchase. The shops were unwelcoming, and the use of a single light bulb made them dark and barely worth the visit. Bread was queued for in towns and butter was non-existent. Chickens were bred at home for both eggs and meat, but I have never eaten such tough chicken in all my life.

The women were bread, cake and cheese makers. They produced a grey, solid version of bread which was served daily without butter or margarine. I never learned to love it. I believe I dreamed about fresh bread with lashings of butter. The cheese was a non-matured type called *brunsa*, a basic curd strained through muslin and eaten immediately. In later years, when we managed to get the boys making cheese, much interest was shown in English cheese cultures, particularly those matured for flavour.

Another delicacy offered for visitors was pig's trotter in aspic jelly. On one occasion Angela and I were invited to eat with a village family and, as usual, we were the only people eating at the table. The meal was set in the front (best) room and we were seated like royalty. We were then waited upon by the lady of the house and her children. As if that wasn't embarrassing enough, we were heading into stormy waters. I shall never forget the arrival of the pig's trotters. They arrived amidst smiles and excitement from the children and undisguised pride from the lady of the house. I was horrified when I caught sight of the content of the two plates of food. In fact, I fought the first signs of nausea when I spotted a lump of pale-skinned, hoofed flesh sitting in yellow gunge. Eyes met mine over the table and dared me to reject it.

The kindness of the family and our inbuilt manners wouldn't allow us to offend. Luckily, by this time, there was a little trick we'd learned. I always kept a surgical glove in my pocket into which I could secrete unwanted food, thus avoiding hurt to the wonderful, generous host families. A trotter in aspic jelly was one step too far for both of us and I declared I would turn vegetarian for the remainder of the visit. I'm ashamed to say that two of that particular pig's trotters went uneaten. The meat, however, slipped from the bone with ease and plopped into a surgical glove. The gloves were intended to shield us from AIDS but they certainly came in useful at the dinner table. We couldn't give the meat to the boys as they were incapable of keeping secrets.

Much ado was made about drinking home-made *suica*, especially by the menfolk who distilled it in their back yards. The clear, plum-based liqueur was potent and, in my view, disgusting, but in the early years much pressure was put on me to partake. Romanians have a way of feigning disapproval over refusal about such matters. However, as the years went by, I noticed Tori always refused alcohol and was never chastised. When I asked how she got away with it she told me, that ladies of a certain age were excused the vagaries of potent drink. Needless to say, I never drank it again.

One day, when Angela and I had been in the village for many weeks we had a lovely surprise. Adrian ran into the camine with a call of excitement. 'Come quick! Come quick!' he gabbled unintelligibly and dragged me by the hand into the boiling hot sunshine. Dorin was not far behind and I believe Ionelle and Gheorgie brought up the rear.

Angela and I watched in amazement as a massive four-by-four, left-hand drive vehicle swept up the drive in a flurry of dust and came to a halt right beside us. We waited while a man and woman got out and at first glance, we noticed they were clearly not Romanian. A middle-aged couple with beaming smiles stood in the oppressive sun and extended their hands in greeting.

'Are you English?' the foreigner asked. I agreed we were and waited for him to introduce himself. It transpired that Dr Jan Broeders, together with his wife Yvonne were working for the Dutch Red Cross on an Aid Programme in Vaslui County. Jan was a special-needs doctor in his native Holland and regularly volunteered his expertise to the Dutch Red Cross. Over the years we were to become good friends and the longer I knew Jan, the more respect I had for his ethos and working practices.

Jan told us he'd heard a chance remark in Vaslui about two English women working in a camine in Giurcani. He was curious to find out which organisation was supporting them, so he and his wife came to find out. He was shocked to discover that we were two lone voices, working in a wilderness.

Angela and I had seen no one except the Romanian villagers for weeks and we were excited to have visitors who spoke English. But better was to come. Jan suggested that as we had no official organisation to support us, we should spend the coming weekend in Iasi with his team of eleven Dutch volunteers. He offered us rooms at the hotel where he and his volunteers lived and promised us a fun weekend away. How good that sounded. We had experienced a huge amount of shock and sadness during those first few weeks, so 'fun' sounded too good to be true.

It was with interest we watched Jan charm the director that day. She smiled and entertained him and his wife to coffee and biscuits and made an invitation for them to visit at any time after personally showing her visitors around the camine. Jan made many visits to Giurcani and in later years, he welcomed the camine director to Holland to learn from the work he did with special needs children. Sadly, no changes appeared in Giurcani.

True to his word, Jan arrived the following Friday to collect us and Angela and I left the village for the first time in over a month. We were like a couple of kids. Jan told us he had worked in Romania for many months and had set up support projects in five camines. His volunteers were all special-needs teachers working with children five days a week, while living in a hotel in Iasi. How lucky they were.

When we arrived at the Hotel Moldova in Iasi we were amazed by its facilities after our weeks of deprivation. We each had an ensuite bedroom with hot and cold running water and a clean double bed. The fabric of the hotel was dated and tired, but we hardly noticed.

We were introduced to the Dutch volunteers who spoke excellent English and were welcoming, if a little bemused by our situation. We spent many hours chatting about our experiences and discovered theirs were similar. However, they had Jan and Yvonne for support, and all had experience of special needs children. We really liked them, and I stayed in touch with two of them for many years. One eventually married a Romanian guy and had a happy marriage with three children.

A tour of the city was offered, and it started next door to the hotel. We'd noticed the impressive, turreted building which was, we learned, the Palace of

Culture. Inside, it had rooms with displays of art and museum pieces, all set around a grand staircase. It seemed odd to us that only one, or sometimes two, light bulbs graced the impressive chandeliers. A single bulb made the place gloomy and almost impossible to view the treasures. Jan explained that electricity was expensive and even public buildings had to make savings.

I loved Iasi. It was the first time I'd dealt with a tram system and I found the need to consider tramlines, as well as traffic, a bit scary when crossing roads. The city had a dazzling array of churches, each with the ornate interior found in all Orthodox places of worship. We admired tree-lined avenues, visited a zoo and strolled through a well-maintained park. However, although we enjoyed the day, it was impossible to ignore the poverty and downtrodden people. It made me sad. Dacia cars were the only family vehicles and displayed varying degrees of rust. Lorries were so old I doubted they were road worthy, and they belched fetid fumes throughout the city. Iasi kept us fascinated all weekend, although I was surprised to find so much smog after the fresh air of Giurcani.

The fact that we had access to hot running water and a shower was a treat, but when we discovered we would be living on Dutch food, brought overland by Jan for his volunteers, we were in heaven. They produced jars of thick chocolate spread and cream biscuits and cheeses. Fresh fruit, cake and many other delights were in plentiful supply. It was wonderful. We spent time between each other's rooms, exchanging backgrounds and sharing jokes. Surprisingly, all the volunteers were receiving their full salaries while working in Romania.

We went out to dinner on Saturday night. Jan and Yvonne chose a smart restaurant in another part of town, which was attached to a hotel. I don't remember exactly what we ate, (there is a diary blank,) but I do remember the attentive service from staff and the friendship of lovely Dutch people, which we appreciated so much. We were like dried-out sponges, soaking up hospitality and the fun of being in touch with English-speaking people, if only for a short while.

On the Monday morning Jan offered to show us some of his projects. We visited three camines supported by the Dutch Red Cross and were staggered by what we found. Under their care, each had evolved into childcare facilities near to European standards. The Dutch volunteers were doing an excellent job with the children including physiotherapy, food programmes and medical care.

We had a great time with the Dutch Red Cross, and I saw them many times after our first meeting.

Life trundled on. June slipped into July and by early August we were preparing to return to England. I think, on reflection, our three months in the camine were worthwhile, as some progress was made. And when I left those children that first summer, I already knew I would return. Something about the older boys had crept under my skin and the injustice of their lives kept me awake at night. Angela felt the same and at some point, we hatched a plan to return for Christmas.

We left the camine with certain changes in place. Many of 'my children' were being fed a regular diet of baby food and some were showing signs of improved health. A few had learned to sit up and two had made efforts to crawl. Angela had similar successes. But I was worried that all the progress we'd made would be lost if the bottles of milk regime was re-instated. I was tentatively confident that some of the women might continue our work, as they had come to understand our motives. But would the director allow the routine to continue? Now was the time for a little faith.

Leaving was heart-breaking. I watched those older boys wave goodbye and sobbed. Had we done harm? Had we shown them something we couldn't sustain? Had we raised expectations only to dash them? I couldn't answer those questions any more than I knew what the future held.

Chapter 9

'The volunteers gave us stuff but we had to give it up when they went home.'

Gheorgie – a survivor of the camine in Giurcani

Back in the real world it was difficult to slip back into what used to be the normality of my life. Over the three months I'd been at the camine, I had grasped a passable version of the Romanian language and I'd even started thinking in Romanian. When I arrived home, occasionally I needed to pause to find the right English word. Ridiculous! However, I had no trouble adjusting to a more interesting diet and never once hankered after village food.

My own boys were pleased to have Mum home and we enjoyed a few days catching up on hugs and all their news. Friends on the Isles of Scilly arranged a welcome home BBQ for me, but sadly, I was fog bound in Penzance and unable to enjoy it. As the locals say, 'that's island life'.

Before I ventured into Romania, I'd accepted a job at Eton College, which was due to start in early September, nineteen ninety-one. I was to be rather grandly named a 'Dame' and the boys would address me as 'm'Dame'. How was that going to fit into life after the vagaries of Romania? Could those two worlds be any more different?

I'd grasped the basics of my new job at interview and knew that I was about to enter a privileged lifestyle. However, I had no idea just how remarkable that lifestyle would be.

My welcome at Eton could not have been warmer. My housemaster, James Cook, introduced me around the campus and the first few days before the boys arrived, was a whirl of dinner and drinks parties. The house staff, who were to be my responsibility, appeared friendly and I hoped they were good at their jobs. As it turned out, all apprehension was groundless and my integration into college life was seamless, if a little overwhelming.

The boys returned for their autumn term or 'Michaelmas Half' as it is known, and I was thrust into a whirl of teenagers who bubbled with noise and enthusiasm. I settled into my new living quarters and felt confident I was going to like my job.

An important bonus of college life was the opportunity to travel in and out of Romania during the generous school holidays. Angela was now a mature student in Kent, having decided to leave the world of commerce. This was to be her legacy from working with the children of Giurcani. Mine was continuing to visit the children in the belief that something good would come out of it. I could see no point in putting my aspirations into a timeframe because the work would take as long as needed. I would continue travelling to the village while I felt I was achieving something positive. Perhaps it was as well I had no idea that three decades and many thousands of pounds worth of fund raising later, I would still be returning to those skinny, dark-eyed children.

Angela and I felt the Christmas visit to Romania was successful, and it was also fun. Our flight was yet again many hours late and we arrived to a snow packed land, with temperatures below freezing. We knew we had no chance of getting to Giurcani that day, so we trawled the hotels but found there was no room at the inn. In desperation I dragged a reluctant Angela into the smartest hotel I could find and announced to the amazed receptionist that we would be spending the night in the plush foyer. Spoken English gave kudos in those early years and no objection was raised. We were at least warm and safe. Didi had arranged for us to be met at Birlad and our telephone call meant the arrangement was hastily adapted to the following day.

When we arrived in Giurcani I was excited and neither of us could stop smiling. We visited Maria to enquire if we could stay in 'our rooms' and hoped all would be well. She grumbled a little but rapidly put her hand out for the rent money, while Nicu welcomed us with a beaming smile. We had bought a bottle of spirits on the aeroplane which we gave to them before hurrying to the camine.

We made a polite visit to the office to wish the director festive greetings and gave her coffee beans which we knew was her weakness. She agreed we could spend time with the children. Her welcome may have been barely warm, but the children's joy and surprise were unforgettable. We had packed seventy small gifts in a large canvas bag and were determined those children would celebrate the first Christmas of their lifetimes. We found two other English volunteers were also spending Christmas in the village and they too, had brought festive items for the children, including a Father Christmas outfit and sticky paper to make paperchains.

We all made that Christmas as special as possible for the children. New cots had arrived. A group from Kent and Marks and Spencer had sent bundles of goodies too, so the camine had a festive spirit, if only in small amounts. The camine director stayed away for three days so there was a relaxed air about the place. I was camera happy as I wanted to photograph the children's first Christmas for posterity. Chocolate covered faces beamed into my camera and warmed my heart to bursting point.

The volunteers made the most of the few days of festivities and we played charades and card games which amused the older children. We sang carols and encouraged the older children to sing along. There was a lot of hand clapping, I remember. The happiest moment for me that Christmas, was discovering the children were still receiving their sieved baby food. Alleluia.

Every time I visited Giurcani, a new need was identified by Dorin who always had his eye on progress. A playroom was created by Dutch volunteers and educational toys, walking aids, wheelchairs and money for food and medicines were provided by the English. More new cots, flooring, clothes, a washing machine and washing powder arrived – the list was endless, but there was a noticeable decline in volunteer visits. Dorin updated me each time I arrived, and I knew him to be reliable. I teased him that one day he would be the Mayor of Giurcani.

The extension to the building was completed at a snail's pace, but eventually it was finished. I could hardly wait to see the cramped camine conditions improved. Now, each child could have their own bed or cot. Jane Clarke was anxious for me to photograph the completion of the building work on behalf of Marks and Spencer. She, like me, was excited by the termination of the appalling condition. I could hardly wait for the grand opening. While Jane waited in Norwich, I arrived in Giurcani just as the final touches were being put to the building. The countdown began.

I should by that time have been less trusting of a system and individuals who lacked both humanity and shame. Had I learnt nothing in two years? Sadly, the director, or those in power above her, admitted another twenty children into the camine to fill the extra space. Not what we had hoped for.

At the end of my second year at Eton and during my fifth visit to Giurcani, I realised other volunteers had ceased to return to the village. I had become a lonely, one-woman crusade. If the task looked daunting before, it was now off the scale of unachievable. Many nights were spent awake as I tried to find a way forward without other volunteer support. By now, I was staying regularly with Didi and Tori Rotaru, rather than returning to the home of Maria, mainly because it was a friendlier environment and the food was good, too.

I had become deeply attached to those three teenage boys. Adrian, Dorin and Gheorgie worked harder than any men I'd known. They spent hour upon hour hoeing the land and planting crops; they fed the animals, fetched and carried for anyone, washed the camine floors and laundered the clothes which they hung on wire fences to dry. And poor Adrian had to work in the director's home, too. The reward for all their labour was minimal amounts of food and no thanks for anything they did. But it was noticeable that no one ever beat them when I was around; one small victory, I felt. I believed those boys, more than any others in the camine, could have managed to live outside of institutional life if only a small wind of opportunity had passed their way.

Over the years I enjoyed deeply rewarding times with those lads. They heaped spade-loads of joy on me each time I visited. I also loved the days when I took the small children out into the sunshine and the boys joined me, sneaking away from their duties and keeping an eye open for the wrath of the director. The lads enjoyed the crayons and colouring books I brought for the younger children, each taking great care to colour between the lines. I could hardly watch Dorin as the concentration and dexterity he achieved with just two digits brought tears to my eyes. That lad never allowed his disabilities to impede his progress in anything. I was so proud of him.

Each visit I took gifts such as balsa wood airplanes, footballs, bubbles, tee shirts and caps, footwear, and jumpers – all manner of things to perk up the children's lives a little. It was heart-breaking to realise some had missed their childhood and their adult lives held no promise of anything good either. No one wanted them and no one cared if they lived or died. Well, now I cared, and dozens of friends were at home to support me.

Often the three boys talked about wanting a life outside the camine and exuded a longing you could taste. They told me they saw kids in the village return to their families after school, and noticed families at weddings, all taking care of each other. No one beat village kids, they told me. But I knew they had no hope of being fostered or adopted. No one wanted uneducated teenage boys with spots and health problems.

Camine children were stigmatised by Romanians, just as illegitimate children had suffered in the post-war years in Britain. I was one of those children 'born on the wrong side of the blanket' as it was quaintly known, and I knew how it felt to be shunned for things that weren't your fault. Around this time, I believe I nurtured a germ of an idea to help those boys. Not a fully formed idea but something that niggled at my brain and itched to get out.

I travelled in and out of Romania, sometimes three times a year. I sampled all the seasons and celebrated Easter, All Saints Day and two Christmases in the village. Every time I took as many gifts as I could carry, and always money to meet the necessities for the children. Friends sometimes came with me, curious to see the project that had almost taken over my life. My younger son Robert visited to see what had lassoed his mother. Everyone who visited was welcomed by the children and everyone went home wanting to help.

The welcome at Didi and Tori's home was also warm, and the friendship grew each year. I regularly visited Didi's school children to admire their success and ensure they had the basics for learning. It was a joy to notice 'my three boys' had started to visit the Rotaru home, too. They did small jobs around the house and garden in return for a generous plate of food and kind words.

The great joy of taking hundreds of photos over many years is the way they jog the memory, especially the happy occasions when the people of Giurcani invited me to join family celebrations. During one of my early visits, when my understanding of the language was limited, I was invited to attend a christening in the nearby village of Pecan. A time and place were agreed for meeting the family and I waited as instructed. Eventually, a tractor of gargantuan proportions chuffed up the road, and aboard the heap of metal sat the grandmother of the baby, leaning on a wheel arch with a large bunch of flowers in her hand. Opposite her was the child's mother holding the special baby who was resplendent in ribbons and a white knitted shawl. I can't recall who was driving the monstrosity, but it drew up alongside me and hailed me aboard. I was a little taken aback but entered into the spirit of the occasion and travelled on the towing hitch to the nearby village of Pecan.

When we arrived at the church we were greeted by friends and other members of the family who'd travelled ahead of us, either on foot or by horse and cart. Together we entered the church and stood in readiness for the ceremony. I noticed the priest was rather rosy cheeked and a little unsteady on his feet. It became apparent he was the worse for drink. The baby, who was no more than a couple of months old, was undressed down to her nappy in readiness for the blessing. A bucket of water was already placed on the stone floor and as we gathered around, the priest proceeded to dunk the baby right under the water, three times. I was petrified he would drop her or even drown her due to his liquor-fired enthusiasm. But apart from some loud wailing, the child was none the worse for the experience.

Another occasion that springs to mind was a wedding Angela and I were invited to during our first visit. We had nothing to give to the happy couple apart from American dollars, so we shared the agreed amount and set out to join the celebrations. But embarrassment lay ahead as we mistook the bridesmaid for the bride, and donated our generous gift to the wrong lady. However, unable to right the mistake we danced the night away and ate copious amounts of food. Neither Angela nor I have a very developed sense of rhythm and we caused much amusement as we attacked the local two-step with gusto. There was singing and more drinking until the dawn came up. We had a wonderful time.

Every time I visited the camine, the boys reiterated their desire to change their lives. The only realistic option ahead for them, from the government's perspective, was a transfer to an adult institution. I knew that would be the end of their dreams. I had visited a couple of those establishments with the Dutch Red Cross and could never allow the boys to be incarcerated in such a place. But where was an alternative?

Sadly, as each year passed, I knew the boys' fate was moving ever nearer. They were too old to be in a camine for children and each time I left, I wept for them, always fearful they would be spirited away before my next visit.

Over the years, it became obvious to me that much of my work in the camine was stagnant. My efforts were spread too thinly and were being undermined when I returned home. The task was too vast for me to make an impression alone, and a new approach was required if I was to continue my work.

I discussed my concerns with Jan Broeders and Didi and both agreed, I was right. The initial influx of help had dissipated, and the old regimes were easier for staff to manage. Much of our push for new methods was shunned. Except, I noticed, the children that Angela and I had spent so much time with, were holding their own. Some were eating in the dining room and all were taken from their cots each day for play and stimulation.

I noticed the donated contents of the playroom gradually disappeared. Little by little the toys and books went missing and soft toys and wall decorations were nowhere to be found. 'They wore out,' I was told. On one visit, the washing machine and tumble drier that I had provided a couple of years earlier, had broken. I was willing to have them repaired and gave the director the money needed to get the job done. But the money and the machines disappeared. The television bought for the older boy's salon disappeared too, along with a CD player intended to amuse the bed-ridden children. Another time the horse had died, from starvation I was told, and they were struggling to collect clean water from the well. The children were drinking contaminated water. Life was grim.

There was, however, one bright spot for me. One year, when I visited, unannounced, I was met with a sight in the village that reduced me, yet again, to tears. For there, outside the village school, and walking in crocodile formation, were six of the children I recognised as those Angela and I had put are heart and soul into saving. The children were supervised by one of the women from the camine who smiled with delight and engulfed me in a bear-hug embrace.

Those puny children I had taken off bottles of milk were right before me. Not only were they walking, but they had smiles and hugs for me that melted me quicker than the summer heat. What a joy! I had continued to work with the same children each time I visited and knew some were close to walking, albeit with difficulties from their disabilities. What a wonderful sight that was. Livio, Sandu, little Adrian and others were forging a life for themselves and I floated on air for a couple of days. I could hardly wait to tell Angela when I returned home.

During moments of despair, and there were many, I told myself to count the blessings and not to dwell on what I saw as failures. A French lady once told me, 'In Romania we do as we can. We are like a dripping tap.' I took that to mean little steps should be celebrated. And celebrate I did. I praised the staff for their excellent work and thanked them for staying true to my aims in my absence. Other areas of the camine were not so encouraging.

It was always a joy to be welcomed back. Catching up with the older boys was a lengthy business, as they wanted to relay every single happening since my last visit. A woman had been sacked, a foreign visitor had called at the camine, a child had died or a village wedding had been celebrated. All these things impacted on their lives.

For me, the welcome in Didi and Tori's home was an essential part of my survival. They were amusing, educated and most of all warm and caring. I knew their family and they knew mine by proxy. I learned much about their lives under the communist regime and the horrors of Ceausescu's rule.

Chapter 10

'I've been told that I could easily have learned to read and write if I'd had hands and feet.'

Dorin - a survivor of the camine in Giurcani

My job at Eton College was a whole world apart from Giurcani. My Housemaster was a philanthropic man and tolerated my passion for Romania with good grace. He also nurtured me through the pitfalls of college life.

My role as Dame involved running the house of fifty boys and eleven staff. I was responsible for the health and wellbeing of the boys and supporting them at sporting occasions, including the wonderful fourth of June rowing regatta. Attending social occasions within the college such as dinner parties, coffee mornings and drinks parties were weekly occurrences and I regularly helped to entertain parents and visitors.

I enjoyed so many memorable occasions at Eton, including lunch at Windsor Castle prior to attending the Order Of The Garter ceremony in St George's Chapel. The invitation came from the parents of one of 'my' boys who was a pageboy to the Queen. There was a close connection between the castle and the college and three times each year the Eton Dames were invited to coffee by the wives of the Knights of the Garter. My first attendance was a somewhat timid affair, however, like so many events at Eton, those occasions soon became commonplace.

There was, however, an occasion when my housemaster was shocked by my behaviour and his disapproval revolved around a sporting event. It was a wet, cold day and I'd been standing on the rugby touchline for more than an hour, spurring the boys on to glory. However, that year my Walpole House boys lost in the final of the House Cup and I was overheard to say, *'Never mind boys – it's only a game'*. My housemaster was mightily unimpressed. *'My Dame!'* he exclaimed. *'Never has such a sentiment been heard on the playing fields of Eton!'*

I lived in a beautiful apartment on the third floor of Walpole House with views of Windsor Castle. My sitting-room window looked onto a glorious garden which was colourful during all seasons. However, in nineteen-ninety-two, I watched with horror as Windsor Castle burned. It was a monstrous sight, and everyone was sad for the Queen.

After a few years of visiting Giurcani I became increasingly disillusioned. There were so many other disasters occurring around the world and fund raising for Romania had become difficult.

I tried to help the village school in Giurcani with much needed books, pencils and paper. Simple things, but when some of the children attended school in the morning and others in the afternoon to share the meagre resources, the need was patent. I was impressed by the quality of the children's work, despite a woeful lack of resources. Didi Rotaru imparted his knowledge with huge enthusiasm.

Didi didn't need to tell me about the difficulties he faced at his school because the need and deprivation told its own story. However, with typical Romanian patience he was resigned to waiting for things that were unlikely to arrive. One day he shared his dream to erect a metal fence around the school and playground, and his excitement for the project was hard to ignore. I thought it a bizarre way to spend charity money, but I listened to the reasoning. I knew Romanians were obsessed with fencing their homes and wondered if this was just a personal desire, rather than a necessity.

Didi explained further; the playground was used by men as an area to drink alcohol and often as a lavatory. He feared for the health and safety of the children. He also felt the kindergarten children were in danger of running into the road and being injured or worse, by a horse and cart. He said secure fencing would exclude trespassers and he could start projects with the children, including sports projects in the school holidays. Having promised myself I would listen to local views and never draw comparisons with life at home, I was coming around to the idea. I trusted Didi and if he said it was an important issue, then who was I to disagree? However, the cost of metal fencing for such a large area was phenomenal. I had to get my thinking cap on to find ways to raise the money.

I made friends with four other Dames at college and they quickly took an interest in my work. After seeing my photos and hearing stories about the children, they offered to form a committee to raise money for the project. I took the opportunity to discuss with them the various problems in Giurcani including Didi's request for a metal fence. After bouncing their views around, they agreed it would be an advantage to have a secure compound for small children. They also felt that school holiday programmes could be a benefit to the village. We decided to make the fencing part of our goal, along with books and other resources.

I went to see Poppy Anderson, the wife of the then Headmaster, and shared my aspirations with her. She listened intently while I poured out my story and questioned the aims, structure and goals of my work. She agreed to help. When people of influence offer support, it encourages you to hold on to your dreams. A renewed injection of enthusiasm put me on the road to helping Didi's school.

Lady Jenny Acland was married to the Provost of Eton and meeting Jenny set in motion additional fundraising on a rather grand scale. Jenny invited me to join an 'International Ladies Club' which she was in the process of setting up at Eton. She explained that when her husband was in post as British Ambassador in the United States during the time of Ronald Reagan, she had created a similar group in Washington. Jenny told me they regularly debated world affairs and gave money to worthy causes. I liked the sound of that, although I wasn't sure how the label of 'lady' would sit on my shoulders.

The international group was formed, and we met alternate months, each meeting being held at a different venue. These ranged from private embassy houses in central London to the most memorable, the private apartments at the Tower of London. It was a strange feeling to watch the Beefeaters from aloft in the tower; I felt a voyeur of the grandest type.

Jenny suggested I should be the speaker at the inaugural meeting of the club which was to be held in the Provost's Lodge at College. I was terrified. I knew that other members included foreign ambassadors' wives and friends of the Acland's. One other Dame, my friend Kit Anderson was invited to join the membership and when the big day arrived her advice was, *'just tell it like it is'*.

After my talk and slide show to that large, attentive group of ladies, I was asked to speak at another meeting the following month. The Jane Shaw Society is an historic club for women at Eton and dates back over many centuries. The society was originally formed in recognition of the male-oriented environment at college and the need for women to support one another. It was thought that they, too, would be interested to hear about my work. I felt privileged to be a small part of it.

Soon, word of our work in Romania spread and it led to an offer from the women of Eton to send gifts to the women in Giurcani. I was asked to prepare guidelines for suitable gifts which I was happy to do, particularly as I was due to visit the village again for Christmas.

That year I took with me an array of small, beautifully wrapped gifts for the village women. The dynamics for distributing everything was kindly arranged by the Rotaru family and Tori had prepared a list of the households we should visit. Didi was my guide when we delivered the Christmas treats around Giurcani by horse and cart and he translated the good wishes sent from England. There was deep snow, as usual that year, which made the delivery extra special. For many village women, it was not only a surprise to be singled out for a gift, but also the first gift they had ever received. It was humbling and I remember it as a poignant moment that spurred me on to achieve even more for those lovely people.

Another outcome of my introduction to Jenny Acland was a grand music recital performed in College Chapel in aid of Giurcani. Jenny, too, became a staunch supporter of my aims and had the ability to open doors for me. The Eton choir and orchestra rendered an amazing concert of music by Romanian composers for which hundreds of tickets were sold to both parents and locals. I've never forgotten the joy when I discovered how many people were prepared to support the camine. College Chapel was full to bursting and the shimmering lights, the smell of candle wax and tentative chords of the orchestra as they tuned up for the event is something I will never forget.

Angela came to visit for the occasion, and we ached with excitement during the evening as the talented orchestra and choir filled the chapel with spine-tingling sound. It was moving to see the Eton boys, all from such privileged backgrounds, playing and singing their hearts out for 'my children.'

Sir Anthony and Lady Acland generously hosted a drinks party after the concert and invited everyone into their beautiful home for bubbles and canapés. Here, staff in traditional black and white uniforms moved gracefully among us, never leaving a glass unfilled. A silver chalice was placed on the vast oak sideboard in the hall and at the end of the evening it was brimming with twenty and fifty-pound notes. I was deeply moved. Close to three thousand pounds was put into the charity bank account the next day. As a result of that evening, I was able to pay for the fencing Didi so desired, and also winter shoes for the camine children, books and pens for the school and play equipment for the nursery school in the village.

My small group of supportive Dames met most Saturday lunchtimes at a local pub called the Pineapple. Here we discussed many things, including life at Eton for women and our fundraising ideas for Romania. (When news leaked to the boys that 'Dames' were setting foot in a pub, we became known as 'The Pineapple Dames'.) Apparently, we were the first Dames to ever confess to frequenting a pub and also the first to be seen in public wearing jeans. The boys loved it – they described us as 'proper people'.

News of our fundraising spread throughout the college and the Roman Catholic priest, an artist of some repute, made us a remarkable offer. Within his collection of works were two fine watercolours of College Chapel and Lower Chapel and he offered us the opportunity to create limited edition prints from the originals. He suggested we could sell them to parents, old boys, and associates of the college.

We took a risk. Spending charity money is more worrying than spending your own, and when we researched the process, the cost of the printing was substantial. We speculated on the number of people who might buy prints and decided to go ahead, trusting that old boys and parents would support us.

We took time and care to ensure the colours and quality of the prints were perfect and in due time, five hundred limited editions prints arrived from the printer. Luckily for us, the pictures were popular with boys leaving school that year and we sold 410, which I believe is considered a good effort in art circles. The prints raised over five thousand pounds and I was able to put more essential items into the village school in Giurcani. The money provided paint to improve the interior of the classrooms, a new floor in the entrance lobby and several new windows. It also kept the bank balance healthy.

Later that year, some of the boys in Walpole House raised money at the Eton Summer Fair for my project. I had a quantity of towels printed from a primitive drawing done by camine children and the work of art was turned into yet another money-making tool. The boys sold tea- towels at the fair and their enthusiasm was redolent of barrow boys in the East End of London. Roll up, roll up. More money came our way.

The boys often came along to my apartment to look at the most recent photos and chat about progress. Unexpectedly, in 1993, three of the senior boys asked if it was possible to volunteer in Romania for a short time during their coming gap year. I was surprised but thought it would be a great experience for them. Over the coming months, Didi arranged for them to teach English in both the primary school in Giurcani and the secondary school in the nearby village of Pecan. The boys would stay in his home for which they would pay board and lodging.

I remember how impressed Didi was to learn that one of the boys was a godchild of Prince Charles and was also the nephew of Camilla. Didi was well-versed in the happenings with our Royal Family and this visit took place after the high-profile press offensive on Charles and Camilla. Another boy on his way to

Giurcani was the child of a famous private banking family. But Romania is a great leveller and from the minute they arrived, all were equals.

The boys travelled out with me after their final exams and I stayed for a month to settle them in. I have very fond memories of those weeks. I watched Eton boys wash their smalls in a bowl of water in Didi's back garden and drape them over a wire fence to dry. My heart warmed when they slipped into a game of football with the older camine boys. They settled quickly and embraced the locals with ease.

After several happy years at Eton College, changes arose around my personal life as I planned to get married to a wonderful man. Eric lived and worked in Gloucestershire and I knew our life together precluded my job at Eton. So, after five wonderful years ensconced in the bosom of Eton College, I chose to move on with my life. I'd been a single mum since my sons were young and the decision to share my life with someone special outshone all the benefits bestowed by Eton College. Eton and her people were superbly generous to my project in Romania and also to me. I loved my years on your hallowed ground.

Thank you, Eton College.

Chapter 11

One day the director told us the volunteers were 'communist spies' and we believed her.'

Adrian – survivor of the camine in Giurcani

Eric and I planned to get married the year after I left Eton. We looked forward to many wonderful times but most of all, I wanted to introduce him to the Isles of Scilly. We squeezed in a three-day break and stayed at the New Inn on Tresco, and Eric was enchanted. How could he not be?

On reflection, my life at that time was idyllic. I was in the flush of wedding preparations and my sons were both happy with their own lives. James and Robert were working, and Robert had a girlfriend in Bath. I liked Katherine very much and my fingers were crossed that the relationship would develop into marriage. Some while later we welcomed Katherine to the family, and they gifted us with three delightful grandsons. My eldest son James would eventually adopt a son and have a daughter and a step-son to complete his family. The tally of grandchildren was rising, and I felt blessed. Eric's two children were generous in their acceptance of me, so we had four wonderful children to enjoy. Vikki and Wade would also gift us with another four grandchildren. Could life get any better?

After our wedding in the tiny church in Cherington in Gloucestershire, we spent a year waiting for Eric to complete thirty years of service in the police force. We talked a lot about our future and one day, out of the blue, Eric asked if I would consider going back to live in Scilly. I was surprised, particularly as he'd only visited the islands a couple of times. We were currently living in my family home which I'd inherited from my adopted dad. I had tenants in my house on the islands but that was not a major problem as they had given notice to leave the following month. I took little persuading to return to those blue waters and white sand beaches.

We bought a house in 1998 at Old Town on St. Marys with the intention of turning it into a guest house. It was a stone-built, Victorian house situated on the coastal path at Old Town Bay and the views from the house and garden were breath-taking – you could almost touch the sea. The downside was the amount of work to be done to turn it into a business establishment.

It was a happy time for us. Newly married and with a common goal, we put our heart and soul into Tolman House. Every morning we woke to the sound of the tide, sometimes a gentle lap of water on sand and often a heavy heartbeat of foaming spray, thrown metres high over Pulpit Rock.

During this busy time, I didn't visit Romania, although the village was never far from my thoughts. I made occasional telephone calls to Didi but gleaned little information about the camine.

One day, in 1999, when we had finished the renovation of our guest house and our B&B business was growing, I received a telephone call from Jan Broeders in Holland. He told me he had visited Romania and called into the camine at Giurcani. He apologised that he had bad news but felt sure I would want to know. He'd found the children hungry, badly clothed and lacking medication. He said the camine was filthy, but the most urgent concern was the children's desperate need of food. The director told him money was short, (when was it not?) and her food budget was half of what was needed. I could imagine her lack of concern and Latin shrug – what could she do about it?

I was deeply distressed. My mind filled with images of those children – each one known by name. How could this have happened again? And I felt guilty. I'd been so busy with my own life, I'd failed them. I had to go back.

Eric and I flew to Romania at the first opportunity. For me it was a journey filled with more than the usual trepidation. What would we find? For Eric it was different. I knew that despite all the stories he'd been told over the years, he was concerned about coping with village life. Would he find it easy to be around children with disabilities? Was he ready for filth and hunger and the primitive living conditions? For him it was a step into the unknown and well outside his comfort zone as a police officer.

Eric

When I first visited Romania, if I'm honest, it was just to please Rita. I knew her passion and commitment to the children was a lifetime thing and it was a case of 'join the party or be a wallflower'. We got married after a long wait to be together and I knew that Romania was a big part of her life. I'm sure neither of us realised just how big it would become and I didn't feel indifferent for long. Soon I was sucked up by the depth and breadth of the cause.

My first visit was in 1999 and all the deprivation I'd heard about was suddenly right before my eyes. Nothing prepares you for what you see, hear and smell. Even after thirty years as a police officer it still shook me to the core.

When we arrived in Bucharest, I remember thinking it looked like an up-and-coming city. OK, it had areas of deprivation and there were beggars on the streets, but nothing was particularly different from a dozen other European cities I'd seen.

I knew the journey to Giurcani was not an easy one. It involved seven hours on a train with the hope that someone would be in Birlad to meet us. But nothing deterred my wife. Rita's excitement was palpable. Every time she visited, I was to learn, she felt an excitement in the pit of her stomach but every time she left, she became tearful with a deep grief that almost choked her. I just steeled myself to watch the lady I loved turn herself inside out with grief for 'her kids.'

I'm sure readers can conjure up imagines of the children in Giurcani. It's not hard to imagine the horror of those stinking rooms. However, this story is mainly about three, courageous lads from among that number, and I'd like you to know them better.

Upon meeting 'my three Romania boys' you might be entranced by Adrian's blue eyes or a cavernous 'Norman Wisdom' grin from Gheorgie. You may be taken with Dorin's sharp mind and sharp tongue when he demands to know all about you. But one of the last things you'll notice, is their special needs.

Adrian is the eldest. We discovered he was already twenty when I first met him in 1991. I thought he was about thirteen. He's a shrimp of a fellow with a shock of muddy blond hair and blue eyes, bright and clear as a robin's egg. He's quiet and thoughtful and shy in his manner of speech. In Romania his colouring is usually attributed to Hungarian blood lines, but who knows where Adrian's heritage lies?

In the early years I developed an affinity with his quiet ways and charm. He was always willing to run errands, and nothing was too much trouble. One day I discovered he had a beautiful tenor voice and with a little encouragement, he sang Romanian folksongs. He was eager to learn English songs too, which he learnt by rote from my own dubious renditions.

In more recent years, Adrian's desire to sing has passed and he has put away other childish delights such as colouring books and puzzles. To be truthful, these days, he resembles a small, wizened old man. A hard life and decades of malnutrition and deprivation have taken their toll on Adrian. I fear he may not live to be a great age. He suffers from frequent headaches and poor teeth; numerous dental extractions and painful treatment have resulted in his fear of the dentist. He now has few teeth left in his poor gums to get a grip on the meat he so enjoys. But still, he smiles that gappy smile that tears at my heartstrings.

103

Dorin comes next in age. He was nineteen when I arrived but looked much younger. He has physical disabilities but a scalpel-sharp brain and deserved the opportunity to go to school. When Didi offered him reading classes as an adult, he had no heart to study and feared he would be laughed at by kids. He's constantly enquiring and never accepts half a truth or half a story.

Gheorgie is the youngest and the least able of the three. He has a kind face despite his rather large ears and wonky teeth, and he smiles from morning till night. He doesn't like to be rushed and too much hustle and bustle gets him agitated. He loves feeding the chickens and geese, collecting the eggs and shutting the fowl in the coop at night. He takes delight in the birth of new animals and spends time grooming the horse. He gets cross with Adrian for drinking alcohol and raises his finger to admonish him, rather like an angry parent.

All three of the boys have been given encouragement to speak about things they remember so that I can tell their story. I want their voice to be heard and much of their life has been documented in the writing of this book.

Chapter 12

'They make you wear clothes with numbers on in Husi. I was in Room 11 so I was only allowed to wear clothes with an 11 on.'

Gheorgie - a survivor of the camine in Giurcani

Dorin

I don't have any memories before life in the village of Giurcani, although I've learnt in recent years that I lived with my mother in Vaslui until I was two. Until Rita came to Giurcani and rescued us from the camine, we never even knew how old we were. When Rita and Eric got our paperwork from the authorities, they discovered our birthdays and every year we get birthday cards from them and have a drink to celebrate.

I want to tell everybody about the place I knew as home for twenty-six years of my life and why I was still in a camine for kids when I was in my twenties. I was a good worker you see, and my labour came free of charge. For that reason alone, I had a value, just the same as Adrian, Dan and Gheorgie and the others. That's why we weren't sent to an adult Institution.

The camine held something in the region of seventy-five kids of all ages. We were all classed as having learning disabilities. (I think that's what the volunteers called it anyway.) But all we knew back then, was that 'we weren't quite right in the head' and 'couldn't live out in the community.' The staff told us we were 'mad'. Strange as it may sound, that wasn't of much

105

consequence to us. We just accepted life as it was. I've got extra problems 'cos I've got no proper hands or feet, but I manage, and I can do most things, often better than other people.

The most important things in our lives, back then, were the need for food (we were always hungry), managing to avoid another beating (they came thick and fast), and the constant worry of how much work was in store for us on any day of the week. And of course, the bloody cold Romanian winters. We have mountains of snow every year. Winter was always a worry, especially for me 'cos I had no winter boots to fit my stumps and so they got red raw with weeping chilblains. When you haven't got proper hands or feet you get bashed about a bit. Sometimes my stumps were so cut and sore I had to stay in bed.

All the days were the same back then, work, hunger, beatings and the occasional laugh when we managed to get one over on the staff. Maybe we'd grab a miserable bit of meat when it was thrown into the soup. The days just came and went. The camine was a shit place, I suppose. Everyone worked hard, except the kids who were tied to their beds and the others in cots.

A boy called Constantin used to smash the glass in his salon window and then cut himself with the broken bits. I remember he did it one day when a volunteer was playing with a kid in the same room. Constantin just sliced his arm, real deep, and then started to cut his legs to shreds. The volunteer screamed for Rita 'cos she used to be a nurse and she came in with a box with a cross on the lid. The thing I really thought strange was she put on rubber gloves before she tried to clean up Constantine's wounds. I've never worked that one out to this day.

Rita told the director that Constantin needed to go to hospital but when she came to take a look at him, she said there was no need for that. Anyway, there was no transport to take him to Birlad so he had to manage the best he could. Rita had some strips which she put on to some of the cuts. We had to help her

106

by holding Constantin down as he fought everyone he came in contact with. And he used to bite like a dog. Dan sat on him and he's big. After the strips were put on, Rita bandaged his wound and then the director said he had to have his hands tied behind his back so that he didn't pull the bandages off. Rita was really shocked.

Nights in the camine were tough 'cos you couldn't sleep for more than half an hour at a time. It used to get dark and quite spooky 'cos we'd have no outside lights, and all the inside lights were switched off or there was no electric. But there were always loads of noise and lots of shadows.

There was always screaming from the small kids' salons, I suppose because of their growling hunger or from lying in the stinking piles of shit in their cots. They'd cry and nobody ever came. Eventually they'd stop screaming and sleep a bit. The older kids, rampaged around beating small children, lashing them to the beds and doing unmentionable things to them. It was the same thing that happened to me when I was little, and nobody saw any harm in it.

One day Rita caught us at it. She was so angry I've never forgotten it. That was the first time anyone told us it was wrong. Now I'm grown-up I can see the harm in it, but back then it was just done for amusement. Stuff like that used to interrupt your sleep 'cos you had to look out for your own safety. As I grew older, I was one of the groups giving out the punishment, being top dog, but in my younger days, life wasn't easy for me with no hands and stumpy feet. But it made me strong and some say it made me gobby. I'm never lost for words – not me!

I've been told that I could easily have learned to read and write if I'd had hands and feet. My wonky body is what made them stick me in a camine. My only problem seems to be a lack of schooling and opportunity. There's nothing wrong with my brain!

But I told Rita, nobody had opportunities in our village back then, so I'm not on my own there.

I'm told I was a cute little kid and during my first year or so in the camine the director used to keep me in her office while she worked. I remember she shared her biscuits with me. I used to crawl around the floor and play with pens and things, but I guess eventually I grew too troublesome. By the time I was four years old she released me to fight my corner among the bullies in the main wing.

Kids were divided into sleeping salons according to what they could do. The volunteers said the rooms were stinking. I've even seen them breathe into a hanky 'cos they thought it was so bad. I can't say I ever noticed. It was just the smell I grew up with.

It didn't take long to see what would happen if I didn't learn to walk on my stumpy feet. Up to that point I'd shuffled on my backside gathering the filth and dust from the floors as I went. It made my arms hurt and even bleed as I used them to navigate my way around. But I was determined to get upright no matter how hard it was or how long it took. Learning to walk was important to me so I could grab my share of the food. I saw what happened to kids who had their food stolen. They got really skinny and couldn't walk. They had to stay in cots all day and all night with a bottle of milk thrown at them every now and then. I wasn't going to be one of them. I'd seen loads of them die and get buried in the churchyard at the back of the camine.

I also taught myself to use the lavatory. I didn't want to be one of the stinking kids who sat in their own filth all day. Wiping my ass isn't easy with no hands - I'll leave you to imagine how I do that!

I learned to stand up on my stumpy feet by hanging on to the babies' cots. I used to slide along sideways, despite the pain from the bleeding chunks of flesh that I call feet. Sometimes, when I was lucky, I'd be given a pair of trainers that were huge, but I was able to stuff my feet into.

The worst thing, even worse than deep snow, was tramping through the shit that surrounded the outdoor lavatories; they're holes in the ground used by kids and staff. Even volunteers had to use them and as there weren't any doors, just three brick walls around a hole, it caused us kids much amusement. We used to burst into applause when they achieved their goals! It amused me that even visitors had to use the same lavatories we did.

Of course, I never learnt to wash my fingers or stumps, water was too precious for that and stomach problems were common; vomit adding to the stench in the camine. My bleeding feet got infected more times than I can remember. Most times I didn't get to see a doctor and the scabs kept weeping and falling off – or I picked them.

I grew up used to nasty comments, threats and beatings. They were part of everyday life for us older boys, those who actually got outside the living block to work in the fields. I grew up to be strong, partly because I learnt to steal food from other kids. I reckoned I was entitled to it as they stayed indoors all day doing nothing and I had to go outside and work. If I could learn to walk, I thought, so could they. Not that I would have changed places with them.

Mostly the women turned a blind eye to my antics, but from time to time I'd catch them on a bad day, and they'd beat me hard. I always laughed, no matter how much they hurt me, 'cos I saw how mad it made them.

The camine director was a strong woman. The women and us kids were afraid of her. But I knew how to get the staff in trouble if they were shitty to me. I'd tell tales to the director and then stand back and watch the results. She would really shout at them and I've lost track of the number of staff I've seen her sack. There were always loads more women in the village who wanted jobs.

Always someone wanted to earn regular money 'cos there was no other work. The women learnt to respect me, in a small way.

The director spread all sorts of information around the place, true or false – no one ever knew. Instructions had arrived, she'd tell us, from the powers on high. 'If we don't scrub all the rooms with disinfectant in the next week, we would have evening food stopped until further notice.' Another one was, 'anyone caught nicking food will be sent to Husi.' Now Husi was the dread of all the older kids. It was an institution for cronky adults and had a fearsome reputation. I used to think I'd run away if they sent me to Husi. Anyway, we still managed to nick a few chunks of bread when her back was turned. She often used to sneak home early and take Adrian with her. He had to do her housework and feed her animals. She never paid him but sometimes gave him wine. Rita thinks that's why he has a bit of a drink problem now he's older, but I wouldn't like to say.

One day the director told us the volunteers were 'communist spies' and we believed her for a few days. It was only in later years that I realised the boss-lady spoke no English and couldn't translate anything the English said. Despite her best efforts, it didn't take long for the foreigners to win us over with the stuff they brought, and we loved the attention they gave us.

Adrian

I knew I shouldn't have been in Giurcani when I was already grown up, but no one told me to go anywhere else, so I stayed. I'm a good worker. Even the director said that, and I think that's why she kept me at the camine. I used to go to her house and dig her garden and sweep her paths. She used to give me a bottle of beer or some wine if I worked hard all day.

I was in charge of the camine cow which was kept for milk. Every morning I had to take the cow down to the village where it was collected by a man who took it to graze on the hills with other people's animals. When they came back in the evening, I had to milk it and take the bucket of milk to the kitchen.

Sometimes we had pigs, too. I loved the baby ones and I used to take a long time when I was sent to feed them. Sometimes I would get in the pen with them. They smelt nice and were always warm. Even in winter.

I can't remember a time when I wasn't at the camine. Like most kids I was there 'cos I'm handicapped. I'm not sure what that means exactly, but I never went to school and never had a family like the kids in the village. I don't think I missed having a mum and dad. I didn't think about it much. Sometimes when I was beaten, I used to wonder if my dad would have beaten me, but most of the time I just got on with my life. I never get beaten now. Rita and Eric would never allow anyone to beat me.

I never worked out how the volunteers could bring so much stuff and just give it away to us kids. They gave stuff to people in the village and to the school. I thought they must live in some magic place where anything they wanted just appeared. That probably meant they had so much, they didn't miss what they gave to us.

Not that we kept anything they gave us for long. Whatever the foreign people gave us was always taken away as soon as they left. The staff stole things when no one was looking and threatened to beat us if we told the director because they would have lost their jobs.

The director could have anything she wanted, of course. Once, the English brought a bike for me. It came on a lorry and I was dead quick to learn to ride it. I whizzed through the village – up and down – up and down. Everyone shouted, 'Go, Adrian! Go faster!' I thought I was a king, flying around with the wind making my hair stand up like a cock's comb. But soon it was taken away. Someone said it was sold in the next village. I never had a bike again.

We never had enough food. Someone told me that's why I'm so skinny. I've never caught up my proper body weight. During the daytime when the cow was grazing, I had to hoe the fields and make sure the crops were good for the year. In the summer it was hot as hell – out in the field hoeing, hoeing, hoeing. My back used to ache, and I had permanent blisters on my hands. But when I looked at Dorin I thought, if he can manage, so can I. Working made me strong. I can work all day long in the fields without getting tired.

I often get really bad toothache and I've had lots of teeth removed. I can remember once when I was in pain for over two weeks - it kept throbbing and throbbing. I begged the director to let me see a dentist, but she told me to bear it like a man. I don't think she wanted to waste money on me. In the end I dug the tooth out with a bit of metal I found and that hurt.

I've made lots of visits to the dentist and it is never good news for me. Rita says the Murgeni dentist is not very clean. I've never noticed really. Everybody who needs treating sits in the surgery, leaning against the wall and watching some other poor sod in the chair. Rita says the dentist uses the same instruments for each patient without cleaning them properly. She seems to think that's not very nice. The dentist does wash his hands from time to time, under a cold-water tap, but there isn't any soap.

If you want to have a painkilling injection you have to visit the pharmacy across the road and buy the anaesthetic and also get the syringe and needle. I never had a painkiller until Rita arrived. This is not something many Romanians can afford. Every time he gets hold of me the dentist hurts me. I haven't got many more teeth to cause any problems, so that's good, isn't it?

I liked it best if I could drive the camine horse and cart, but that didn't happen often. I always had to fetch the water for the camine 'cos we had no well of our own. The groundsman and me took the horse and cart outside the village to a water hole twice a day. In the winter the hole was frozen and I had to beat it with a stick to break the ice before we could drop the bucket down. We'd fill up milk churns with water and bring them back on the cart. It could be a freezing cold job. I never had any warm clothes and only sandals on my feet. We never had socks till Rita looked after us. Now we wear socks every day and I have three pairs of footwear. I've got wellington boots, trainers and sandals. I forgot – I've got indoor slippers, too.

Sometimes, but not often, cook at the camine would let me stand in the kitchen to get warm. The smell of the soup always made me hungry. I used to like watching her make the bread. They were big loaves that she cooked in the oven over the fire. My mouth used to water and I'd dream of being able to eat a whole loaf instead of the miserable bit we were given with soup. Sometimes I'd steal from other kids. It wasn't nice – I know. But I bet you'd have done the same if you'd been me.

Rita used to tease me and sing songs. I still know the English words to 'Row, row, row the boat'. Umm... I remember we also played with balloons. I'd never seen a balloon and when my one went bang, she really laughed. She wasn't even cross. She blew some air into another one for me. And there were magic bubbles. You just blew at a stick and they floated in the air. I never worked out how that happened. We used to play clapping games and I always clapped at the wrong time. Sometimes Rita laughed until she cried. I didn't understand that either.

We used to have crayoning books and I loved learning to draw between the lines. Angela helped as well. We'd stick the pictures on the camine walls, and the women used to say things like, 'you're behaving like a kid. Five-year-olds do colouring, not stupid great lumps like you.' I must have been about nineteen at the time. But I didn't care. I loved my pictures, and they gave me a good feeling inside. No one could take that away from me.

113

I used to take Rita to see the baby pigs sometimes, and the calves. Umm...I remember one day it was time to slaughter a pig and the men came and cut the pig's throat in front of her. She was a bit upset but it's the way we do things in Romania. It's always a good day when we kill a pig. Rita said she couldn't bear the smell of the blood that ran through the dust near her feet. Everybody (well, not us kids at the camine – not very often anyway) got a small piece of meat when a pig is killed. It's a real treat. The men burn all the hair off the pig with matches and then strip the skin with sharp knives. They eat it straight from the pig. I thought Rita would be sick that day, years ago. I often wonder what they eat in England. They have lots of funny ways, the English.

One year I remember Rita came for Christmas - and Angela. We had never heard of Christmas. We made decorations from pretty paper and we put them up in the playroom. There was a present for every kid in the camine that year. And we had a shiny tree with decorations on it.

Gheorgie

One day they came and took me away. Giurcani wasn't much of a place to leave but I was sad. I had friends there and no one told me where I was going. Um...it rained that day I remember because I'd put my wellington boots on in the morning to take out the rubbish and the shitty bed sheets from salon 4.

Mostly there were two kids in every bed, so I used to wait until they both had a crap and then I only had to change the sheets once. Viorel, who worked in the laundry, had the job of taking the turds out of the bedding, so he was grateful.

Well, those wellington boots never went with me. The director took them off me and told me to walk in the mud in my plastic sandals. Can you believe that? She said the new place could provide me with footwear and I wasn't taking hers.

114

I travelled in a white van sent by the Direction for the Protection of Children in Vaslui. I remember another kid went with me, but I didn't like her. She was crazy and tried to steal everybody's food which she stored in her knickers – even when she had her monthlies. Nobody wanted to steal it back after that. She was a screamer at night, and she used to give me headaches. I often get headaches you know. You'd have thought she was being eaten by wolves some nights. The staff said it was nightmares, but nobody cared. Adrian used to hit her and tell her to shut up. If she took no notice Ionelle used to threaten to stick his thing in her. That usually did the trick. Anyway, that day we were bundled into the van and I never said goodbye to anybody. Adrian was out with the cow and I didn't know where Dorin was.

They took me to Husi which is a place for handicapped people. I didn't know how old I was, but I knew I wasn't a kid anymore. I knew I was handicapped, but not mad. Most of them in Husi were mad.

When we arrived, I was taken up to the second floor and we passed a woman running down the stairs with no clothes on. She was being chased by a very cross bloke who was yelling at her and threatening to tie her to her bed for a week if she didn't come back. I felt afraid. She didn't stop and I could see her out in the garden from the high-up window. She was screaming as if she was about to die.

I hated it at Husi. The women were much worse than the ones in Giurcani. At least some of the women there were nice to you if you did exactly as they told you and worked hard. But in Husi it was really bad. I first had to share a bed with a skinny bloke who kept shouting in his sleep and kept me awake for nights. He used to wave his thing at me and ask me to do horrible things to it. One day the staff changed him for an old guy who snored and sometimes wet the bed. I would wake in the morning soaked in his pee. It wasn't nice.

I was given a job washing the floors. Not just in my room but all the rooms on the second floor. I had to carry buckets of water upstairs after fetching them from the water tap on the ground floor. They made me put some liquid stuff in the water which they told me was to stop fleas. It smelled disgusting and it made the skin on my hands come off. It was hard work washing floors all day. As soon as you thought you'd finished some bloke would have a crap in the corner of one of the rooms and I'd have to start again. If he'd smeared it on his skin, more often than not I'd be made to clean him up, too. I used the water from my bucket 'cos I couldn't be bothered to go all the way back down for clean water. Not to wash a bloke who would do it all again tomorrow.

They made you wear clothes with numbers on in Husi. I was in Room 11 so I was only allowed to wear clothes with an 11 on. I could recognise an 11 easily but often the best clothes were grabbed by other blokes. I've never been one to push in a queue. In the winter there were never enough warm clothes. I needed warm clothes 'cos I had to keep going outside to get water, but no one listened. I was always cold, and my feet were always soaking wet from the water I carried. I got bad coughs too. I hated that place. I missed the animals in Giurcani and Dorin. Adrian was my friend, too. I like working with animals, but I didn't like cleaning floors.

One day I was told to undress and leave my clothes on the bed. They gave me an old dressing-gown to put on and it had no belt, so I was embarrassed when my privates poked out.

Nobody said why I had to take my clothes off. I wondered if I had to see the doctor. I'd told the women for weeks that I had sore eyes. I hoped at last I would get some medicine for them.

Eventually I was pushed into a transport van with six others and we were taken to another camine. There wasn't any medicine and I still get sore eyes all these years later, even though I have medicine now. Rita makes sure we have money for my eye drops. They told me at the hospital in Birlad that the damage is forever; that's 'cos nobody listened to me when I was younger. Nobody ever listened to me in the old days. I hope I don't go blind when I'm old.

'Dorin

Once I had learnt to walk, I was given duties every day. The director went easy on me at first, asking only that I helped to serve the meals or make her coffee in a jug and bring it to the office. But after a while I was sent out to hoe the fields with Adrian, Dan and Gheorgie and this was really hard. When you don't have hands or feet, it's not easy to use a hoe but I manage well. And I can drink soup from a spoon.

Chapter 13

I dug my tooth out with a bit of metal I found and that hurt.'

Adrian - survivor of the camine in Giurcani

After the telephone call from Jan Broeders, it felt as if we were preparing for a mercy mission. Eric and I flew to Bucharest from Heathrow and Jan Broeders arranged for us to be met at the airport by the manager of a Romanian charity called the Joseph Foundation. He explained they carried out humanitarian work in the city of Iasi. True to the promise, we were met by a jolly Romanian who took us by car from the airport to spend a night at the Foundation house.

It was here that we first met Daniela Cornestean who worked as a child psychologist for the charity. We stayed in her office on a bed sofa that first night and awoke the next morning to a hoar frost sparkling on the cabbages outside our window. I remember we overslept and Daniela, who was waiting to start work, was too polite to knock!

Daniela gave us a guided tour of the house and introduced us to the children and the work she did. She explained the Joseph Foundation was licensed by the Romanian Government to arrange adoptions both inside and outside of the country, and it was part of her role to assist with the fostering and adoption programme. It was usually the babies and toddlers who attracted families, she told us, but the older children who arrived from the streets were not often lucky.

We heard how the chosen children awaiting adoption were cared for and loved by staff during those anxious months. Prospective parents visited as regularly as they were able and when the complicated administrative processes were completed, they took their precious child away to a new life. Children started a fresh life in many European countries, including the UK.

The Joseph house was full of happy, healthy, smiling children. And it was so clean! Many of the children were nursery age but there were also older ones who went to school daily. All were having their lives turned around by the dedicated staff of this Christian organisation which received money from churches and individuals all over Europe. Of course, there was never enough money to do everything they wanted, but to me it was like a nugget of gold shining in a muddy riverbed.

Another aspect of Daniela's work as a psycologist was her programme with street children. The Foundation offered guidance and support to children, mainly through soup-kitchens on the streets and in extreme cases, children were taken into the Joseph house. Here staff tried to reunite them with their families and after counselling, some returned home. Others were kept at the Foundation home where they were fed, well-clothed, cared for and sent to appropriate schools.

Daniela was also working with Romanian gypsy children. The Romany tradition of marrying children around the age of nine or ten was hard to curtail, even though it fell into conflict with Romanian law. Marriage at such a tender age was a cultural issue ingrained over centuries and Daniela believed education was the only way forward. It was tough going for her, but she appeared to be persistent and thorough. I found the Joseph Foundation an inspirational place.

The work at the Foundation in Iasi was an eye-opener for Eric and me. Until that visit, I thought only foreign intervention was making headway with the problems of unwanted children, but now I'd met Romanians who were working to the same standard as such organisations as the Dutch Red Cross. This work at the Joseph House was, of course, influenced by Jan Broeders.

A huge bonus for us was Daniela's perfect English which made our lives easier but had a detrimental effect on my effort to speak Romanian. I freely admit I got lazy about the language, although when the need arose, I could still hold my own.

Daniela wanted to set up a fostering service for the children in her care, those for whom there was no hope of a reunion with their families. This project entailed not only finding suitable foster families but monitoring the progress of the child, and also paying for the child's food and clothes. Eric felt moved to help and told me he'd decided to approach the Rotary Club on the Isles of Scilly to see if they could help with funding.

All too soon it was time to say our farewells to the lovely people who'd impressed us with their generosity of spirit and hard work, and by mid-morning we'd set out in our rented car for Giurcani. I was fearful about what we might find.

(The Romanian government banned foreign adoption two years after this visit and life became really tough for the Foundation as they relied upon donations from generous, prospective parents from Europe. No more foreign adoptions meant fewer kids would have happy homes. Some of the Foundation's funding was raised by Jan Broeders in Holland but the generosity of foreign parents was imperative if the work was to continue. But these were problems for another time and at this moment they were doing extraordinary work.)

Our arrival in Giurcani confirmed little had changed in the village. Still the dust swirled, and the flies annoyed. Our arrival was met with huge warmth, but there was a special welcome for Eric too, who was told, *'it was about time someone took care of Rita.'*

Our generous hosts were the only people in Giurcani with whom we could discuss our concerns about the children at the camine. Didi and Tori Rotaru were good listeners, and little happened in the village that they were unaware of. So, our tales of hunger at the camine were no shock for them.

After conversations late into the night we discovered that, not only was the camine suffering, but the whole country was in dire straits. As the camines were at the bottom of the government pecking order, this was where the most radical cost-cutting had fallen. It was as grim as we'd feared.

Eric and I visited the camine the next day and I was overjoyed to meet Dorin and Adrian who were waiting at the gates for us. Word had spread of our arrival and many of the well-known faces were still working with the kids.

Children gathered around us with the enthusiasm of small puppies. They clamoured for attention and noticeably, more children were playing outside which I felt was a good sign. I knew a duty visit to the director's office was necessary protocol and shooed the children away as we made our way to her door. She greeted us with cool hospitality although she was notably warmer to Eric, than to me. No surprise there. We'd brought her a gift of coffee beans to sweeten the meeting and for about ten minutes we played around with niceties.

But I wasn't in the mood for small talk, so I asked the director for her view of the current situation. Was she having difficulties feeding and clothing the children? Had the staff been paid? She answered with a shrug and a 'what can I do' attitude. I asked her how was she managing and what was she most in need of?

When I'd left two years before I knew there was a mountain of clothes stacked in the storeroom. Clothes for all sizes and seasons were stored for future use, thanks to the generosity of supporters in Kent. There should have been enough to last three or four years. However, when the director allowed us to look in the storeroom, we saw the cupboard was bare. My shock was apparent, but she shrugged some more. We left her office that day with heavy hearts.

We took a tour of the salons. Many of the women gave us hugs and told of their fears for the future. They agreed standards at the camine had slipped but told us it was not only the camine kids who were hungry; they had hungry families at home and no money due to a three month back-log of unpaid salaries. These women were scared about the future and rightly so. No volunteers had been there since my last visit, they told me. (I knew Jan had visited but said nothing.) But the really bad news was the discovery that Gheorgie had been sent to an adult institution. My worst fears had come to fruition and I was unable to gain any news of him.

The children were indeed a sorry sight and although they hadn't reverted to the really bad old days of 1991, they were far from fine. Many had skin complaints and weeping sores on their faces. Some had hacking coughs and they were all thin and poorly dressed. There were very few smiles and I could see malnutrition was again on the march.

Eric and I discussed the possibility of raising money to feed the children, but our worry was how to administer the programme. My lack of trust in the camine director and government bodies meant I would never give them money.

Didi had a good idea. His son Dragos, who I'd known and liked for many years, had a friend with a car which was a rare commodity at that time. And they came up with an offer for us to consider. The proposal was that once each month Dragos would go to Birlad to buy food in bulk from a warehouse and deliver it to the camine to feed the children. It sounded a good possibility, and as it was the only one we could think of, we agreed it had many positives points and duly thanked them. Together we devised a list of essentials to be purchased and went to discuss the plan with the director.

You would have thought we were offering her an ice lolly. Her attitude was nonchalant at best although she agreed the list was appropriate, adding one or two other items that she felt essential. On our insistence, a paperwork trail of the purchases would be created, but we still worried we had no hands-on involvement. Out trust was again tested. But just as we thought we had solved one problem, another crawled out of the woodwork.

There was talk around the village that the camine might close in the foreseeable future. No one knew why, although all would become clear. Naturally, the women were worried about their jobs, miserable as they were. I had sympathy with them but also had other concerns on my mind. I knew if the camine closed the oldest children would be sent to adult institutions; they'd probably end up where Gheorgie had already been dumped. A visit to the director was no help as she had only a shrug to offer on the subject.

I was already feeling the benefit of having Eric by my side. He had an unbiased perspective and both feet firmly on the ground. At times, my head was outvoted by my heart and that was not a good way forward. We heard village gossip that foster homes might be found for the younger camine children and this time I knew the talk of camine closure had foundation. I'd learned, a few months earlier, that the European Union had stipulated Romania must 'clean up the orphanages' if their bid to join was to have any chance of success. I tried to tell myself nothing happens quickly in Romania, certainly not anything concerning the government, but this set alarm bells ringing for me.

Did this mean, at last, that the older boys would end up in Husi?

The boys were worried too. The grapevine was working, and they'd obviously been talking about it between themselves. I believe it was the fourth day of our visit when three of them came to us with a request. But what an enormous request it was! They asked if Eric and I could help them have a little house of their own in the village. They wanted somewhere they could lead independent lives.

Adrian told me he was *'sick of all the screaming kids in the camine and being hungry.'* He wanted to live a proper life with his friends. I have to say it came as a shock, although looking back, I have no idea why. Why had it never crossed my mind to create an Independent Living Project for the more able boys?

Eric and I gave them no more hope than we would think about it. We both realised what a huge undertaking it would be and a life-long commitment, too. I had never envisaged being surrogate parents to camine children, but Eric told me later he knew in that instant that somehow, we would find a way to do it. He said it was 'written all over my face.' I can't comment about that. We left a substantial sum of money with Didi for the food programme and returned to the UK.

Eric and I returned home not only with heavy hearts but with three projects to consider instead of one. I was determined to provide food for the camine and somehow, we needed to purchase a house for the boys before they were lost to us for ever. Eric also wanted to help with the Joseph Foundation fostering programme. The projects would need huge amounts of money and although the charity bank balance was healthy enough to fund the food campaign for the foreseeable future, as it was an open-ended need we had no idea how much money would be required.

Back home in Scilly we decided to approach two groups of local people – the Methodist Church of which I was a member and The Rotary Club to which Eric belonged. We offered to give each organisation a talk and show slides about our work. Together, we shared our hopes with everyone, not only about the hungry children and the fostering programme, but also three boys and their desire to have a house of their own. And the response was amazing. With great generosity, people got behind us. Our friends Neil and Rose immediately arranged to sponsor Adrian, while Mo and Lee took Dorin under their financial wing. Friends Tony and Deanne together with Eric's mother agreed to help with a monthly donation and all that generosity continues to this day.

The fundraising began in earnest. We organised strawberry teas and jazz in our garden at Tolman House, concerts, suppers, sponsored walks and many other things – all done with huge amounts of love and support from caring people. A black-tie ball also brought in much-needed funds. The island community and visitors alike became involved, and it was a humbling experience to receive money given with so much faith. I felt moved that everyone trusted us to do the right thing for those children. And so, we did.

The projects fired people's imagination. Hungry children will soften the hardest hearts and we also had offers of clothes and toys. Many people told us they supported us because we were personally carrying out the work. It was interesting to hear views about the larger, well known charities, as many told us they felt too much money was spent on administration. For our small effort, every penny raised went to the kids.

We rang Didi to see how the arrangements for the food deliveries were coming along. The list we'd approved included flour, milk powder, eggs, butter, sugar, cheese, honey from Didi, chickens and yeast. It was agreed that items could be varied should the director make a request that was reasonable. Didi told us the first delivery was less than a week away and I felt a unique excitement that only comes when attributed to the children of Giurcani. All the paperwork would be kept for our inspection and although we knew the system wasn't fool proof, it was the best we could do from a distance. We put our trust in the Rotaru family, knowing they had never let us down before.

With the food project underway and the continued generosity of the island community and its many visitors, we eventually decided that buying the house for the boys was a reality. We contacted Didi and asked if he could source a suitable house for us, and also consider who might make suitable 'guardians' for the boys. We asked him not to tell the boys about our decision at that stage.

It was around this time Eric and I decided to formalise the fundraising. We were, at times, holding substantial amounts of money in a charity account but felt the time had come to account for it on a more formal basis. And so, we applied for charity status from the Charity Commission. We decided to call our new charity the Joseph Foundation and there were two reasons for our choice of name. Firstly, Daniela's employers at the Joseph Foundation in Romania agreed to allow the house to be bought in their name as foreigners were not allowed to buy land in Romania, and secondly, it seemed less complicated to use the same charity name as we hoped, at some time in the future, to give support to Daniela's work, too.

We were delighted to be given Charity Commission status for the Joseph Foundation in the UK.

We visited Giurcani during the spring of 1999 as we needed to check on the feeding programme, view a house Didi thought might suit the boys and also find out what the future held for the camine. Daniela kept us up to date via email about her fostering programme and we took money, not only for her project, but also for the continuation of the food programme at the camine.

As we approached the village my stomach did somersaults. I feared the boys would have disappeared, however, Adrian and Dorin met us with huge smiles. They were their usual exuberant selves and Dorin was full to bursting about local information and gossip which, apparently couldn't wait! I noticed several gaps in the salons which proved there was a movement of children underway. Where they had gone was a mystery as the director, true to form, was not forthcoming.

Eric and I had prepared an outline for the Independent Living Scheme, aiming to make it safe and sustainable. We were under no illusions about the mammoth task ahead although we didn't yet want to tell the boys. We discussed our ideas with Daniela and Didi who were both on board for the project. They threw various ideas around and we dovetailed all the

128

ideas to make a finished document. Didi was most insistent that we realised this had never been attempted. He told us no one wanted camine kids. So, trailblazers we were then!

We were delighted to find the paperwork for the feeding programme was in order. Dragos was pleased with the wages we gave him and told us he was happy to continue the food deliveries for the foreseeable future. Good news indeed. We even extracted a grudgingly positive remark from the director. But we didn't need her to tell us there was a marked improvement in the children; we saw it the moment we checked them out. We also asked the women about the arrival of the extra food supply and they told us, they too could see improvement in the children. Eric and I thought it likely some food had gone astray, but perfection is hard to achieve in Romania.

The main task for that visit was to initiate a process for choosing and releasing children from the camine into our care. Daniela had professional experience of placement of children, and she met us in the village to assess the group of children I put forward for the scheme. We were all anxious to make the right choices to ensure the project had a real chance of success.

Adrian and Dorin were my first choice of boys. They were well known to me, hard workers and desperate to make a new life for themselves. They had, in my opinion, all the qualities to ensure success. The boys liked Daniela and her vast experience of working with street kids made her the perfect choice to assess their ability. She'd gained their confidence and they had an excellent rapport with her. Luckily, after some psychological tests Daniella agreed they deserved to be on the list. Several other boys were considered but it was agreed most would find it hard to cope outside of the confines of institutional life. Most had difficulties too severe to manage living independently.

Although Gheorgie was lost and causing me much heartache, Eric persuaded me to focus on the children who were still in the camine. I accepted that was sensible but Gheorgie was never far from my thoughts. Among the others we considered was Dan, a tall, well-built lad who was always keen to work. He was a capable boy, even though he had never been to school. On a previous visit Didi and Eric had taken him to visit a shoe factory in a nearby town to watch the process of shoe manufacturing. The owners gave him needles, thread and leather to help him get a small business started in the camine. Dan taught himself to repair shoes and boots and the small amount he charged the villagers made him some pocket money. We thought he deserved to join the project.

I was keen to assess a girl called Lucica who helped me wash and feed the children during my initial three months in the camine. She was diligent and we had enjoyed many happy times using play items intended for the younger children. Nine years before, a small boy of about four or five had appeared in a cot next to the door of my salon - it was as if by magic. He was able to walk, he wasn't undernourished and clearly didn't fit into the regime I was setting up. However, Lucica was thrilled he had arrived in our room. The director had nothing to say on the matter.

The newest addition to my programme was a joy. Instead of sad, sullen eyes peering from a skinny little face, he was nourished and always smiling. We potty-trained him – success created much cheering and clapping, and I introduced him to structured play. But I noticed Lucica rarely allowed him far from her side and he obeyed her every instruction. I began to wonder if she was his mother, but when I asked, the staff assured me that was not the case. They told me Lucica thought he was her little brother and insisted he be known as 'little Adrian.'

It could be expected that I became unshakable after the horrors I'd witnessed in the camine, but many years later something proved that was not so. I discovered that same boy, 'little Adrian' was living in the village, (by then a strapping twenty-year-old known as Petico) and it transpired he was, indeed, Lucica's son. I was deeply saddened and shocked. Not only did Petico know the facts about his mother, but also knew a man in the village who was named to be his father. Petico told me Lucica had been raped and the culprit had, in recent years acknowledged Petico as his offspring. Lucica had been sent to Husi when she became pregnant and returned after the birth without her baby. Petico was brought up in a camine in Birlad and returned to Giurcani several years later as 'little Adrian'. The even more shocking news was that Petico was the second child born to her. Lucica remains in Husi today as it was sadly agreed, with her exceptionally low IQ, she was unlikely to fit into the project. No charges were ever brought against the man.

Daniela decided Adrian, Dorin and Dan would all be suitable for the project. It was clear they would need 'guardians' to oversee their welfare; everyone was anxious our lads would be safe and protected from those who may be unsupportive of our aims. Daniela thought that such things as learning to take their medication, (Adrian was epileptic,) being taught to care for their home and managing finances was probably not within their capabilities without support. And of course, they couldn't read or write.

Eric and I had concerns about the villagers as we expected some could be negative towards the project. We worried the boys could be treated unkindly by those who were indoctrinated to despise disabilities. The lads could also lose their possessions which we had worked so hard to provide. In view of this, we decided the right people must be found to oversee their well-being. The lads didn't need anyone to live with them, only to oversee their lives. We wanted someone to keep them safe.

To the best of our knowledge this was a ground-breaking proposal so there was no blueprint to follow. Even today, we have never met anyone who is running a similar project. Many volunteers set up independent living schemes in Romania, but the projects were later handed over to the government to run. We intended to support these boys for their lifetimes.

After a few days Daniela came up with her detailed assessment. In her view, Dan would be the leader of any group as he had the highest IQ. Dorin, despite his physical difficulties was bright and Daniela believed he would offer much to the project. For Adrian, her views were no surprise to me. He had severe learning difficulties but was compliant and a hard worker. For me, Adrian's inclusion was non-negotiable. The three boys had grown up like brothers and I believed their closeness would be an asset to their new lives.

The second evening of our deliberations we received a bombshell. Didi told us he had something to say that could seriously affect our plans. He'd been undecided whether to reveal the news but felt he must. He told us that Dan had recently been cautioned by police for making sexual advances to young girls in the village and the rumour in the village was he'd exposed himself to a camine worker. I was speechless; having known him for so many years this was not only hard to grasp, but a major blow to our plans for him. We talked long into the night, all agreeing such behaviour could jeopardise our chances of success.

We couldn't ignore the facts before us, particularly as Daniela had earlier voiced concerns over Dan's desire to find his family. Unlike the other boys, he was convinced that if he could find his parents, they would welcome him home with open arms. We suspected that to be unlikely and Daniela spent time counselling him on the matter. But she wondered if he would leave the project to search for his roots.

No one wanted the project to start off with major problems and we knew that whatever the facts of the matter, the 'English' would always be blamed for any failures. The accusations about Dan were confirmed by camine staff and within a few days the director sent him to Husi. I was bereft. I felt I'd let another camine kid down. We heard later that he'd gained employment with the shoe manufacturer, which was a grain of comfort to offset the misery of him living in Husi. Later, he disappeared, presumably to find his family and sadly we never heard of him again. I still think of him often and pray he curbed his inclinations and found somewhere safe to live.

It was decided our plans needed to be discussed with the director of the camine and I wasn't looking forward to it but we would need her support for removing the boys from state care. We hoped for some co-operation. Surely, anyone would want the boys to have a better life, particularly boys she had known for more than twenty years? Daniela offered to come as translator and to ensure there were no misunderstandings.

It was an interesting meeting, and we noticed a distinct shift in attitude from the director when faced with Daniela. Maybe it was recognition of her qualifications as a psychologist, (all qualifications hold kudos in Romania) or maybe she was embarrassed by the state of her camine before another professional. Who knows? The outcome was a stern warning from her (to me directly) that 'you'll never manage it and even if you do the villagers will never accept the boys.' We were not deterred by her negativity, but we asked her not to discuss our plans with the boys until they were on firmer ground. Of course, she did. She told them, 'Rita will take you into a house but after a couple of years she will forget you. You will have to live on the street when you can't pay your bills.'

We made an appointment in Vaslui to meet with the Director for the Protection of Children to discuss the project. We needed to know the legal implications and if the authorities would put obstacles in our way. We had no expectation that this would be easy and set off for our meeting in Vaslui with trepidation.

Daniela was dressed in the clothes we called her 'Miss Psychologist' outfit. She looked stupendous in her black skirt, white blouse and high-heeled shoes with a generous helping of red gloss to her lips. She explained the etiquette of such a meeting to us, (we, who wore jeans and tee shirts due to a lack of smart clothes.) Our friend explained the preparation for the meeting was less straightforward than it would be in England. For a start, we had to buy flowers for the lady who was to discuss our case. Secondly, Daniela explained to Eric, there was huge benefit to be gained if he kissed the lady's hand when greeting her for the first time. I laughed, knowing it was considered an act of respect to women in high office in Romania. I announced he should kiss her hand ten times if it got us what we were coming to discuss.

We waited an hour and ten minutes after the appointed time for the meeting. We were seated in a grim concrete corridor in a building still under construction and the head-throbbing noise from a jackhammer prevented conversation. Eventually a sassy young lady dressed in a smart business suit came out of the nearest office door. In perfect English she apologised for the delay and introductions were made. Daniela offered the flowers with a thousand words of rapid Romanian. Then, as we stood in that concrete corridor, my husband stepped forward with his rehearsed greeting. Not only did he kiss the important lady's hand but looked into her eyes and told her he was *'charmed to meet her'* in perfect Romanian. I would have given him an Oscar on the spot! We were invited into her office and the long-awaited coffee was ordered from her secretary.

This senior member of the Child Protection Team told us she had never heard of foreigners taking responsibility for camine children. Consequently, she had no idea of the required procedure. She listened with interest to our plans and clearly found them bemusing. She had no idea of the status of Dorin or Adrian, she told us. The records were unclear. She pondered the question, perhaps they were adults or maybe they were still, technically minors. Enquiries were made. While we waited for her telephone calls to be returned, she emphasised that this would be a commitment for life if we were allowed to take the boys into our care. We agreed.

We discovered the initial paperwork for Dorin was easy to untangle as it was established, he was indeed still a minor. As such, he remained under her jurisdiction. Adrian was more difficult. She told us we had to get parental consent or consent from the Mayor of his hometown before they would release him. Whew… this was not a small challenge.

Vast amounts of paperwork needed to be signed for Dorin, but eventually it was agreed that in our own time we could take him out of the camine. Importantly, she agreed to leave Adrian and Dorin in Giurcani while we tried to progress our plans. We celebrated with lunch in a local hotel, and for the first time I really believed we could do this.

We looked at a house Didi had suggested but felt it didn't quite meet all the criteria. The main problem was its isolated position up a long dirt track which was almost impossible to use in the winter, particularly for Dorin. Didi agreed to keep looking.

Our friend Daniela made several telephone calls about Adrian with the scant details we squeezed from the director in Giurcani and the next day we drove more than a hundred miles to seek out Adrian's family.

This initially looked like a fruitless journey as the man deemed by the local social worker to be his father, denied all knowledge of his son. Luckily for us, the social worker agreed to give consent for Adrian to join our project and duly signed the papers for us. She explained that Adrian's father was an alcoholic and his mother was in a mental institution. So, two boys were ready to go straight into a house when the right one could be found, however we still needed a third boy for the project.

It was soon time to return home to Scilly and we were immensely grateful to Daniela for her support. We took her back to Iasi where she needed to catch up with her own work commitments. Leaving the camine was always an emotional experience for me. Every time I left, I was determined to leave with some dignity, but I never achieved it. It was heart-breaking to wave goodbye to those kids, knowing the life I was leaving them to. But this time there was more than a glimmer of hope for two of them.

On our arrival home we continued to fundraise with renewed vigour. I knew a group of ladies with a wonderful talent for quilting, and one day they asked if I would like them to create a quilt which could be raffled to raise money for the boy's house. I was thrilled with such a generous gesture and eventually, the completed quilt arrived. It was a work of art in vibrant orange a grey and each section had, I knew, been stitched with hope for our boys' future.

We approached two friends who ran the airport buffet on St. Marys and asked if they would display it and sell raffle tickets for us. The footfall in the airport was probably the greatest on the islands. Theo and

Cath were more than happy to help and so the amazing work of art appeared on the wall of the cafe, carefully covered in cellophane. The money poured in from visitors as they came and went from the islands and were tempted by the striking wall hanging. The proceeds came in one pound at a time, but soon we had raised over a thousand pounds.

Chapter 14

We were so happy when Didi contacted us about a house that might be suitable for the boys. It sounded perfect. It was situated on the main road so would not involve the boys plodding in deep mud in winter, it had land and a garden, two rooms and a kitchen as well as two outbuildings. The cost was £3,500 sterling and after much discussion, we felt able to go ahead with the purchase.

Daniela visited the house and agreed with Didi it was perfect, so it was arranged with all parties that the purchase should go ahead. Daniela used the Power of Attorney we'd given her in readiness for this moment. As I was familiar with the geography of the village, I knew the exact location of the house and Eric and I were confident about the opinion of our friends.

Nothing vaguely resembling a structural survey takes place in Romania. It is the ultimate 'buyer beware' experience. Daniela set in motion the notary paperwork which expressed our intentions (using the Joseph Foundation as our intermediary,) and although it sounded straightforward to purchase a small village house, it proved to be a tricky process. However, happily the future of the boys was well on its way.

We set our minds to transferring the money needed for the transaction into Romania. It was simple enough to take cash into the country, but we could only trade in the local currency and lei could not be purchased outside of Romania. For many years it had only been possible to exchange German marks or American dollars for lei, but we had it on good authority from two sources, (Didi and Daniela) that we could now safely bring UK sterling in to buy the house. Due to the difficulties of transporting cash (there was no easy, online banking in Romania) we took the money in fifty-pound notes. I knew Romanian banks were renowned for rejecting foreign currency if it was creased or torn, so we were meticulous about taking perfect notes.

And so, it was another trip to Romania – this time to view the house and pay for it. We also needed to choose a third boy for the project and guardians for them. We decided it made sense to take three boys into the house as four would overcrowd it.

This particular visit was a milestone moment for us both and when we arrived in Giurcani, we received our usual warm welcome from Didi and Tori. The grapevine worked rapidly, and it was not long before Adrian arrived at Didi's house. Dorin, we were told, was waiting for us in the garden of the new house. Apparently, he was examining the garden for suitability to rear chickens. And so, we walked the length of the village to view our pending purchase and found it was everything we'd hoped for. Didi held the keys, on loan from the owner, so we were able to look around. It was clean, tidy and big enough for three boys. The garden looked adequate to make the boys self-sufficient and we were more than pleased with Didi's choice. Now we needed a third boy to make the little family complete. Gheorgi was my choice but he had been sucked into the adult institution system. For the moment he was lost to me but the hunt for him was imminent.

Daniela agreed to come to the village to help interview prospective guardians. This was an important process and we'd drawn up a list of questions as well as a schedule of our expectations. Our wishes for the boys included a healthy diet, medical care, a work schedule and behaviour guidelines. We were looking for someone who understood young men and who could have a sensible, flexible approach to the mammoth task ahead. Whoever we chose needed to be brave. We were looking for someone not motivated by the money we would pay them, someone with a good heart and a desire to see the project succeed.

We were blessed with all of the above when the Manole family shone through for us. Although I knew many village families, I had never met this one, largely because Mariana Manole had never worked at the camine. As far as we could tell, she and her husband Paul had all the qualities we were looking for.

We agreed to pay the family a salary for two years. It was pitched at local rates and would be paid every three months in advance. During the two-year period they were expected to meet our stipulations and standards which were devised to make the boys self-sufficient. We wanted the lads to learn to cook and keep their house clean. We also wanted them to cultivate their land. However, what we got was somewhat different.

Mariana, Paul and their son Daniel, who was away at university in Iasi when we bought the house, were keen to make a success of their new roles. I suspected that part of their motivations was money to support their son's study, but we had no problems with that. They were clear about our aims and promised to protect the boys in any way necessary. However, despite all our aspirations, we were soon to learn yet another lesson about how things are done in Romania.

Before we took Daniela back to Iasi to make the final papers for purchasing the house and to pay the notary, we needed to exchange our sterling into lei. And so, Eric and I set off with purpose to Birlad.

We queued in the CEC Bank in the centre of town for almost half an hour with £3,500 in fifty-pound notes on our persons. The queue shuffled at an endlessly slow rate and I remember how hot it was. We finally reached the teller, heaved a sigh of relief only to be shocked, yet again, by how fast the changes were taking place in Romania. To our dismay, the young lady behind the glass refused to take our fifty-pound notes. Now, she told us, only smaller denominations of sterling could be cashed or exchanged due to the risk of forged notes.

We left the bank dismayed; the problem appeared to be insurmountable. Eric and I stood on the imposing steps of the building, washed with sunshine in a foreign land with no idea what to do next. Eventually we returned to the bank and asked to speak to Didi's daughter Larissa who was a back-room member of CEC staff. We hoped she could help us. When she appeared with smiles and greetings it became obvious, she was unable to suggest a course of action. However, all was not lost for Larissa rang her brother, Dragos, who was now married and living in Birlad, and asked him to come and meet us.

I had become very fond of Dragos over the years. He is a kind, funny and gentle person who works hard to provide for his family. He has many of his father's kind ways and we hoped Dragos would suggest something to get us out of the mire. Soon he arrived, wreathed in smiles and generous with his hugs of greetings. After listening to our problem, he had a suggestion, however it wasn't a course of action we could consider. Particularly so for my retired police officer husband. We listened as Dragos assured us our only option was to go to a black-market exchange which apparently operated on every street corner. He said he would come with us and oversee the deal, but we weren't happy. We were caught between a rock and a hard place.

Further debate took place over coffee and Dragos assured us it was common practice in Birlad. In fact, he told us, all over Romania. He gave a confident shrug and assured us we had nothing to worry about. We certainly weren't going to fail the boys at this stage of the operation so, it was decided, with much trepidation that when in Rome .... we could see no alternative.

As we walked to a less busy street, Dragos accosted a guy who was loitering by a small food shop. We wondered how he knew the man was a moneychanger but after some discussion, the guy agreed to exchange our sterling at that day's bank rate. Further instructions followed. The stranger would meet us around the corner where he had parked his car, and here the secret deal would be done. Eric and I looked at one another and made an agreement with our eyes. It was a case of house or no house, so it was a no-brainer.

We walked in the beating sun across a busy street to the appointed place. It looked like any other street – parked cars, mostly old and rusty, busy people and children kicking an old tin can around.

An invitation was offered to join the guy in his car. Eric and I sat in the back seat clutching our cash while much discussion took place in the front seats. Eventually, a plastic carrier bag stuffed to bursting with lei was produced. Dragos explained that we had to show the guy our money, but not hand it over to him until instructed. The deal was done by exchanging five-hundred pounds at a time, with Dragos checking the lei against our sterling. It was like something from a film. Very cloak and dagger.

Soon, we all agreed that each had the correct amount, shook hands and got out of the car. I looked around, fully expecting the strong arm of the law to touch my shoulder but we waltzed down the street with no consequences, gripping a plastic carrier bag in which nestled thousands and thousands of lei. It was surreal.

The next day we took Daniela to Iasi. I could hardly believe that we were close to putting Adrian and Dorin in their new home. Closer than I ever thought possible. When we told Daniela our story of the money changing, she laughed and said, 'This is Romania. It's normal'.

The paperwork had to be completed in both English and Romanian and Daniela explained the law required us to pay for a translator. At this point the money was handed over for verification by a secretary. The supermarket carrier bag, bursting at the seams with lei, was removed from a rucksack and duly found its way into the notary's office to be counted. The process didn't even raise an eyebrow.

We were both anxious to fully understand the clauses that ensured the Joseph Foundation would keep the house for the boys in their lifetimes. I wanted everything to be secure and legally binding. The translator assured us that all was in order and we were given copies of the paperwork in English while Daniela kept the Romanian version. The transaction was complete. I could not believe it. It had been a roller coaster ride into which Eric, and I had put our heart and soul.

We had the necessary permissions to take two boys away from their lives in the camine, although it was hard to digest this information after years of dreaming about it. Sleep evaded me that night. I was exhausted with the sheer emotion of the moment, but my head would not allow a moment's rest. Everything was churning; lists of household items competed with the niggling strands of fear about what we had taken on. Never had I dared to believe this day would come, despite the hard work we had all put into making it happen. My Christian faith was underpinned in a very special way that day.

We agreed with Mariana and Paul that the boys should spend the first few days in the Manole family home while they acclimatised to their new life. This was going to be an enormous change for Dorin and Adrian and we were anxious to take things one step at a time.

Eric and I took our car to the camine the next morning to collect them. Adrian was called from tending to the animals and Dorin was already speeding towards us as fast as his legs would allow. We told the boys we had business to attend to with the director and left them standing outside the office while we made our way inside.

That lady was not a happy bunny. She used all her powers as director of the camine to prevent us taking the boys away. She had no knowledge that the papers had been signed in Vaslui, she told us. We suggested that a telephone call would confirm it. She needed the boys to work the next day, she said. We couldn't just take them, she added. I have no idea how our conversation was overheard but the next thing to happen confirmed the grapevine was alive and well. Dorin knocked on the office door and announced he was ready to go! Adrian was lurking behind him, less confident but beaming from ear to ear.

We decided to leave the director to make her telephone call and followed the boys to their salon. Very little would be taken. Adrian had a cactus in a small pot, a radio we'd given him the previous year and Dorin had a cassette player and a baseball cap which he insisted was his own property. Technically, the clothes they stood up in were the property of the state, but Eric was adamant it wasn't an issue. I suggested that they said goodbye to the staff but Dorin made a very rude gesture which suggested he wouldn't be doing that. And that was how the boys made their farewell.

Many of the staff came to see them off, calling words of advice and teasing them about being on their best behaviour. I could see glimmers of genuine affection. We drove the short distance to Mariana's house and introduced them to one another. Of course, Marianna knew the boys by sight, but this was a whole new experience for all concerned. They were shy and quiet as they were shown their room. The best thing for them, and I saw their eyes shine with delight, was the enormous meal prepared in their honour. For the first time in their entire lives, they could eat until they were full. I find it hard to write those words, even years later. Imagine tear-stained ink blots at this point. Those two boys had escaped the horror of the camine and had a life to look forward to without beatings or hunger. I was well aware this was a drop in a very big ocean where child deprivation was concerned, but it was a start.

Chapter 15

'I dreamed I could be normal and have a house of my own.'

Dorin –survivor of the camine in Giurcani

Because I am very stubborn, I was determined to find Gheorgie. I needed to trace that lost boy and offer him a better life, too. I was sure he would fit into the project and I couldn't rinse his smile from my thoughts. Luckily, Daniela promised to help us, but it meant we had to run the gauntlet of the director once again. Only she could provide information of Gheorgie's whereabouts.

As expected, she was reluctant to release the information until Daniela told her she would ring the Director of the Protection of Children in Vaslui and tell her some paperwork had gone astray in Giurcani. Hard tactics, but it did the trick.

The state records, reluctantly produced by the director, were sparse but Eric, Daniela, Adrian, Dorin and I set off to Husi where it appeared Gheorgie had been transferred. However, after an hour-long journey, frustration set in when we discovered he'd been passed over to yet another institution and those records were sketchy, too. There was one bright spot to come out of the mistake that took us to Husi as I spotted Lucica, the mother of Petico, sitting on a swing surrounded by a group of other residents. She rushed to give me a hug and I felt incredibly emotional about that poor girl. We'd spent long hours together washing and feeding children and now she was living in this hellhole. I remember thinking that maybe one hellhole was much the same as another, but this felt like guilt playing tricks with me.

We prised information about Gheorgie from the director of Husi and set off on the trail of yet another forsaken institution. I wondered if we would ever find him. If our information was correct this time, he was living about forty miles away in an isolated hamlet. So, we travelled the dust roads in silence. I was crumpled with worry, afraid that he would no longer be at that establishment, either. Could he be lost forever? Children were passed around like parcels and no regard was ever given to their needs.

Suddenly, the enormity of our quest was dawning. Was I really travelling the wilds of Romania looking for a lost boy who belonged to the state? I watched the ever-present swirling dust that prevented us from opening the car window and stayed deep in thought. Even the boys had nothing to say, seemingly sensing the tension.

There was nothing to see but hills etched with stony pathways leading into nothingness. Mile upon mile of open road until, at last, a building loomed from the barren landscape. It was an old mental institution now filled with older kids from camines and adults of all ages who had nowhere else to be. It consisted of a series of concrete block buildings with a scrubby bit of lawn at the front and looked deserted in the heat of the day.

We found the administration office and told Adrian and Dorin to sit on chairs outside. We knocked and entered when bidden to find a sullen secretary engulfed by a vast wooden desk. She looked up without a smile. Daniela, again dressed to impress, spent some minutes telling the young lady what we had come for. A slightly raised tone suggested she was not being taken seriously, however, eventually the director was brought to see us. He was an interesting man offering smiles and an interest in our quest. I had brought a photograph of Gheorgie and, after consideration, he announced that the boy was in his institution. He sent the secretary to find him. In the meantime, Daniela had a discussion in quick-fire Romanian, presumably about how we might achieve our aim. I noticed much frowning and again the raised voices. But still the director smiled.

While we were waiting for Gheorgie to be found, the institute doctor arrived. Word had spread about the crazy English couple who wanted to take a boy away and keep him for ever. I was unable to contribute to the conversation or meet Eric's eye; I was feeling sick with anxiety. Tears were not far from falling and doubt washed over me like a dark, black cloud. But miraculously, Gheorgie appeared. He was dressed in old trousers and a navy jacket over a bare chest, but his smile was unmistakable. He threw his arms around me and refused to let go. Dorin and Adrian were invited into the office and the three boys were at last reunited.

We knew we had no chance of getting Gheorgie released that day, or even that week, but we agreed to return the following day when hopefully the staff would have some information about how the paperwork could be created to allow him a new life. I also wanted Daniela to have time to speak to Gheorgie and judge his reaction to our suggestion. It was important to me that he was offered the opportunity, but the decision must be his. We said our goodbyes and promised to return.

The following day we went back to see Gheorgie but left Adrian and Dorin with Mariana. They planned to help her with the animals, and we felt it would be good bonding time for them.

Upon our arrival at the institution, we were met with the news that as with Adrian we must obtain permission from Gheorgie's parents for his release. Eventually 'Miss Psychologist' persuaded the director to break the rules and give us the information of the parent's whereabouts.

Daniela and I did our best to make sure Gheorgie understood what we planned for him. We needed to know if he wanted to return to Giurcani, but it was hard to judge how much he had absorbed. He was so excited and kept agreeing with everything we said to him. Yes, he wanted to live with Dorin and Adrian. Yes, he wanted to live in a small house instead of an institution. Of course, he did.

Daniela was anxious to spend time alone with him. She wanted to assess him in the same way she had the other two lads. No one wanted him to be unhappy or unable to cope with life outside of the confines of the system he'd always known. So, we all took a walk and Gheorgie gradually calmed down. He appeared to have a serious talk with Daniela and answered a lot of questions about himself and the things he could remember about Giurcani. He also told us a little about his life in the institution. I wanted to scoop him up and take him home that day, when I heard how he was treated.

Finding Gheorgie's family would have been impossible without Daniela. She used her professional knowledge to ring the mayor's office in Gheorgie's town of birth and made enquiries on our behalf. It transpired that Gheorgie's father and a brother were known to the social worker who kindly offered to meet with us and facilitate the necessary consent. As the village was several hours drive away, we would have to wait until the next day. Another day lost and my patience was strung out like a violin string.

The next day we were welcomed to the Mayor's office by the social worker who informed us Gheorgie's father could be found tending cows in a nearby meadow. The helpful lady gave us some background to the family circumstances which didn't make pretty reading. There were three brothers, all illiterate, and the mother was in a mental institution. It was with some amusement that Eric and I sat in the car and watched Daniela pick her way around the cow pats in her high heels, tight black skirt and professional white blouse. Large sunglasses shaded her eyes and not for the first time, we remarked how lucky we were to have met her.

As it turned out, one of Gheorgie's brothers was in the field with his father. If they were amazed at the sight of visitors, they didn't show it. We watched from the car as they listened intently to Daniela who told them of the opportunity for Gheorgie to have a new

152

life and the need for his father to give it his blessing. The brother, who bore a remarkable resemblance to Gheorgie asked, 'Is my brother so crazy that he can't live with us?' Daniela, having been told of the family circumstances, told the caring brother it would be best for Gheorgie to start a new life with his friends. She told him that the family would be given his address and be made very welcome if they wished to visit. The father was visibly upset and, with tears in his eyes, he agreed to sign the paperwork. We would, it seemed, be able to rescue his son from the institution. A large X was duly made on the dotted line. It was yet another emotional moment for me.

After years of believing Gheorgie was an orphan, I now held knowledge to the contrary. Adrian also had a family. Did that mean Dorin had parents too, I wondered.

The kindly social worker took details from us of the whereabouts of Gheorgie and countersigned the paperwork in triplicate. So, with the necessary paperwork in hand we returned to the institute and made our bid to have Gheorgie released. Luckily, he was just as enthusiastic about the venture as when we left him.

We were all ushered into the director's office where, after a conversation with Daniela, he started the paperwork. It was the first and last time we witnessed a system whereby each sheet of A4 paper used had to be logged, by number, in a file. It took eight sheets of A4 to complete the process and we had to sign each one. All were, of course, duly stamped with the ubiquitous ink stamp found in every business and state organisation in Romania. (Even today the Romanians have a propensity to stamp every document they can lay their hands on!) Rather naively, I asked if Gheorgie should go and fetch his belongings and was told he had everything on his person - in other words, he owned nothing in the world. I was shocked, despite the number of years I'd worked in Romania. Luckily, the staff didn't ask for the clothes he was wearing to be left behind as we had brought nothing for him to wear. That day I watched a young man leave a lifetime of confinement behind him and not one person shook his hand or wished him well. We just walked away with him.

Gheorgie

One day, in Maeliesti, just like most mornings I was sweeping the dining-room floor and laying the tables for dinner. So, I didn't see them arrive. Suddenly a kid I was friendly with said some foreign people with two Romanian kids were talking about 'looking for Gheorgie'. He said they had a photo of the Gheorgie and he thought it was me. I wondered if I was in trouble.

It turned out the visitors had gone into the director's office and the doctor had been seen heading that way, too. After a while, one of the women came to find me and told me to go to the office. Umm…. I started to feel a bit scared if I'm honest 'cos I couldn't think why foreigners would be looking for me.

The first thing I saw was Dorin sitting on a chair outside the office. I'd forgotten how little his legs were. They didn't even reach the floor. Then I noticed Adrian. We all hugged and had a quick chat 'cos we hadn't seen each other for ages. Then the door opened and I was told to go in. My hands were shaking and I nearly ran away. But I was brave. And it was such a shock. Umm... Rita was standing there with some people I'd never seen before and I rushed in and gave her a huge hug. The director said, 'I

154

suppose he must be the boy you are looking for,' and Rita cried. Just like she used to when she had to go back to England and leave us in the camine in Giurcani. I wasn't in trouble after all. I don't really remember much of what happened after that. There was someone called Daniela who was Romanian. I didn't know her but she seemed kind. I was told Rita had married and her husband Eric was with her. He looked kind but he didn't say much.

Rita and Daniela told me they wanted to take me away to live with Dorin and Adrian in a proper house in Giurcani. I couldn't understand properly what they meant. How could I live in a house like ordinary people? With me being handicapped. They came back the next day too and stayed for ages and I said I'd like to do what they suggested. Live with Dorin and Adrian again. But then they said they had to go away for a while. They had something they had to do, I think. They said they would be back soon to take me away forever. I don't know why I couldn't go that day, but I just couldn't. I knew that if Rita said she would come back then she would. But it might be a long time 'cos I knew she had a very busy life in another country. I didn't mind waiting.

A few days later Rita and Eric came to get me. I was excited. I hadn't been in Giurcani for ages and Dorin kept telling me we weren't living in the camine anymore. He said we had our own house with a garden in the village. I didn't believe him but it's not much use arguing with Dorin, so I said nothing. I just waited to see what would happen.

I was taken to Mariana's house. I didn't know her, but she came out to meet us and everyone was talking at once. It gave me a bit of a headache. I don't like it when people talk loudly around me. I always think I've done something wrong. I remember we had a huge meal. Adrian and Dorin had been living with Marianna for over a week and they told me we had this much food every day and always meat and cheese which we never saw in the camines. I think I was quiet that night. It was all very confusing and I couldn't stop thinking about not ever going back to Maeliesti 'cos I had a girlfriend there. I didn't tell anybody what I was thinking. After we'd eaten, we went to look at the new house.

When we got back to Mariana's house there was much excitement. The boys ate a huge supper before Mariana got the hair clippers out. Contrary to me believing Gheorgie brought nothing with him, it appeared he had a substantial infestation of body lice which were duly dealt with.

The following day we found Paul and the boys working on their new home. They'd decided it needed painting inside and outside and they were doing preparation work for the 'paintfest.' Paul said they should take the horse and cart to Murgeni and buy the paint and we followed in the car. The boys got to choose the colours and returned with everything needed to do the job. They had their first lesson in the intricacies of filling holes with putty and painting window frames from Eric. We felt Paul was taking on his new responsibility with enthusiasm too.

We were keen for the Manole family to be involved in choosing the contents for the house and this required a trip to Birlad. It was agreed we would take Marianna and Daniela in the car and Paul would set out early in the morning in the cart with the boys. We expected to hire a lorry to deliver the long list of items when they were purchased.

Shopping with the boys was fun. We purchased everything from beds, mattresses, carpets, lino, a fridge-freezer, a three-piece suite and pots, pans and cutlery. The list seemed endless, but no stone was left unturned to do deals. We included a colour television which was the highlight of the day for the boys. A lorry was hired with the help of our friend Dragos and it made a steady journey to Giurcani, laden like a Steptoe and Son cart.

On the way home we stopped at Murgeni where we purchased chicken wire, a hammer and nails, a spade, fork and wheelbarrow and various other essentials. Every nail was invoiced, and every purchase stamped in triplicate – of course.

We were exhausted but happy. I looked at 'my boys' and felt a swell of emotion. How proud I was of them for their courage, trust and excellent behaviour. But I was very aware of the big tasks ahead. We were all stepping into the unknown with little but trust and faith for companions.

Eric

When I married Rita in nineteen ninety-six, I had no idea that, within a few years I would be travelling in and out of Romania with the ease of a local. If anyone had told me I was also destined to be surrogate father to three young men from a Romanian institution, I would have laughed at the very idea of it.

Rita and I have known one another for almost forty years so our twenty-four-year marriage is based on a long-standing friendship as well as love. Her passion for orphans in Romanian was well known among our friends, many of whom were pro-active in their support. But I must confess I'd always managed to steer clear of all the hoo-ha surrounding the fundraising. Until I married her! It was just as well I had no idea about what was coming my way.

157

Inevitably, when Rita and I became a couple, I started visiting Romania. I was curious, of course, but I also wanted to support Rita's passion for those youngsters. And in that far north-eastern corner of Romania three young men in a camine told us they wanted a 'normal life'. There was something deeply touching about that. 'Normal' to them didn't include a computer or a bike, it just meant enough food to eat each day, a little house to live in and some land to work. Because those older lads didn't have the brown-eyed appeal of younger Romanian orphans and were too old for adoption or fostering schemes, they were largely forgotten. They slowly rotted in institutions. With their broken teeth, under-developed bodies and spotty faces, no one gave them a second glance. Except, of course, my wife.

No one mentioned Romania's bureaucracy either. As a retired police officer I thought I could cope with most things in life. I'm a patient man. But I'd never taken on Romania. However, I learnt quickly and I'm the first to admit Romania is not just a different culture, but judged on its bureaucrats, I wondered if it existed on the same planet as us.

I didn't expect to get sucked through the emotional mangle, either. After all, I was a rufty-tufty policeman. But then I witnessed kids being crushed until every shard of joy was squeezed out of their young lives in Romania's infamous camines - my life changed too. If you've ever seen a grown man scrabble in the dust to retrieve a chicken bone, searching for a fragment of meat, then you'll understand how I got hooked. I thought I'd seen life in all its gory detail during my thirty years in the police force. But no – I'd seen nothing like this.

It's fair to say that I wouldn't have missed our visit. This was the culmination of all the fundraising and Rita's long-held dream for 'her boys'. Our aim was to set three young men on the road to an independent life, allowing them to leave behind the institutional hell they'd known.

For three weeks we watched life-changing events evolve before our eyes with excruciating slowness. We rode a roller coaster of emotions as we fought the authorities for the rights to care for Adrian, Dorin and Gheorgie. How could it prove so hard to achieve something so simple? Every conceivable obstacle was placed before us. Huge amounts of bureaucracy were overcome to release three human beings whom nobody wanted – except us. It is no exaggeration to say we travelled thousands of miles to achieve the essential paperwork.

In the overall pattern of Romanian life our small project barely merits note —particularly when you consider the thousands of children who were left behind. But believe me, if you could see the joy and industry those lads brought with them you would share our delight. When we leave them these days, the usual flood of tears from Rita is absent. We wave goodbye to three diligent, well behaved young men who are a credit to their community.

There were various plans for the house. Over time we wanted to dig a new lavatory and also build a small extension to create a bathroom. Eric thought an electric boiler would be the answer in the long term if we could get water to the property. In the meantime, they would fetch churns of water from the well outside the village. Paul had his own horse and cart so that would not be a problem and Adrian planned to help.

We had a long-term hope that we could build or convert an outbuilding into a cheese-making room and get the boys earning a small wage for themselves. But that was all for the future. For now, everyone was brimming with excitement and high on the whole experience. The boys were ready to leave Mariana's and move into their own home. We, too, wanted to see them safely ensconced in the house before we left.

And so, the monumental day came when they arranged their new possessions, chose their beds and eventually slept for the first time in their lives in their own house. We hung the Isles of Scilly Rotary pennant on their bedroom wall and explained the significance of all the money given by the members and other wonderful people.

But our problems weren't over yet. It is a legal requirement for every resident in each village to be registered with both the Mayor and the police. We duly took the boys along to comply but, unsurprisingly hit a stumbling block. Gheorgie did not exist. We asked the boys to wait outside the police station while Daniela, Eric and I ventured inside where we were greeted with nods and stares but were duly listened to. Dorin and Adrian appeared on their database, we were told, and could be issued with their credentials, but not so poor Gheorgie. 'There is no such person,' we were told firmly. 'He does not exist.'

It was time for action. Eric produced his membership card for the International Police Association (something he rarely does) and placed it on the counter with a smile. This led to deep conversations between the men about the police force and a promise that Eric would send an English police badge to the inspector who was an avid collector of police memorabilia. Suddenly, the issue with Gheorgie did not appear to be insurmountable.

The officers asked for Gheorgie's date and place of birth and took his photograph. Suddenly he became a legitimate member of society. That was yet another case of getting what you need by the back door. Several years later we recognised the importance of having the appropriate paperwork as the boys would receive a small disability allowance, a free bus pass and basic hospital treatment if they had their ID cards. Welcome to the world, Gheorgie!

We wanted the boy's health checked and as I had a long-standing acquaintance with the local doctor, a visit to her enabled us to discuss the issues that were bothering me. I was concerned after the 'Dan affair' about the boy's sexual behaviour. Dr Sualia said she didn't expect a problem. She'd known the boys for many years and had never heard of any issues. She promised to keep an eye on the family and to visit Mariana regularly to check how the boys were settling in.

The boys had blood tests to check for all the nasty possibilities. Happily, they were all given a clean bill of health, apart from Adrian's and Gheorgie's epilepsy and all three boys were anaemic. Dorin crowed that he was perfect and needed nothing. We also took Adrian to the dentist which wasn't a good experience for him.

We still had major expenditure ahead of us. The house needed two wood burning stoves built in both the boys' bedroom and the kitchen. Mariana knew the local stove-builder in Pecan so we gave him a visit. The price was agreed, the money given to Mariana to pay him when the work was completed. We also had logs delivered in readiness which the boys unloaded and stored in one of the outbuildings. I think we must have been exhausted but adrenaline carried us on the wings of the gods.

161

Eventually we had to go home although we wanted to see everything finished and check how the village would accept the boys. But we had to trust those we'd chosen to care for them. The Manole family told us they would complete the painting of the house and oversee that all was well for the boys. And we felt confident that they would. I left the village, for the first time ever, with no tears. Just hugs, smiles and promises to come back the following year. Our wonderful friend Daniela needed to go back to work, too, but we knew Didi would also keep an eye on things. It was arranged that Daniela would visit the boys about every six weeks and email us a progress report.

We trusted all would go well.

Chapter 16

During the next two winters Eric and I turned our guest house into a restaurant to raise funds for the boys. When we advertised that we would host dinner parties and celebrations for islanders we were kept busy as most restaurants closed for the winter in the Isles of Scilly. We hosted the Christmas dinner for Barclays Bank two successive years, we arranged private dinner parties and endless evenings of fun, laughter and hopefully, good food. I was chef and Eric did a sterling job as waiter and front of house.

We continued our strawberry teas with jazz on the lawn each summer, too. It never felt as if the fundraising was hard work. Groups of willing helpers piled jam and cream on scones and poured tea from china teapots. On many occasions we enticed some of our paying guests to join in too. And we poured Pimms in the sunshine while visitors enjoyed the jazz, professionally provided by friends Theo, Cath and other musicians when they were available. Happy days.

Dorin

When we were living in our own house, Rita and Eric visited one year and promised to buy us tickets for the circus which we heard was in Vaslui. I think I was the only one who really knew what a circus was 'cos I'd seen it on TV, but we were dead excited about having a night out. When we arrived on the circus site, which was in a huge field just outside Vaslui, we hung around while Eric queued for tickets. There were loads of people everywhere and we eventually went inside this huge house made of white material. Rita said it was called 'the big top', which made no sense to me.

The first thing I noticed was the camine director and her family who were already inside and sitting in seats near the back. We walked straight past them. I nodded to them and they smiled at us. Eric led us to the very front seats. I couldn't believe that we had the most expensive seats and that no one else was sitting in the row. People are poor in Romania and not many people have as much money as Rita and Eric. There was a huge stage built right in front of us and there was music playing and lots of loud talking from the crowd. There was also a funny smell. I can't explain what it was, but it made me excited.

Suddenly music started playing and the stage filled up with dancers and clowns and acrobats all doing different things and all smiling right at us. We hardly knew who to look at. I loved being at the front 'cos we could see everything. Nobody tall was in front of me. I looked at Adrian and he was staring at the stage with his mouth open. I nudged him to remind him to shut it. He looks really dumb when he does that.

I couldn't stop looking at the dancers. They were pretty girls in blue costumes like the things girls wear to go swimming, but these ones were covered in sparkles. (I'd seen Sue Ellen wear the same thing in Dallas, years ago when Rita bought us a TV in the camine.) The girls had feathers on their heads, and they danced right up close to us. I'd never been that close to so many pretty girls before and certainly not ones with hardly any clothes on. I looked at Eric and he gave me a wink. I think he liked the girls, too.

Suddenly a girl appeared with a huge snake wrapped around her body. Rita said it was a python and she looked scared of it.

164

I'd seen pythons before on TV but had no idea how big they were in real life. The girl put the snake down and did some juggling and I noticed the snake moving towards us. I looked at Rita and I thought she was going to run out of the tent. She looked so scared, especially when the snake started to come over the edge of the stage and very close to where we were sitting. I wasn't scared, but I was pleased when the girl noticed it and put it back round her neck. Later Rita told me how pythons curl around people and squeeze them to death. I'm glad I didn't know that at the time. Adrian couldn't take his eyes of the girls' legs. Gheorgie just liked the snake. We had a brilliant time and after the show we all had hot dogs from a man who was cooking them in a van.

I knew I had been born in Vaslui, but I didn't know exactly where. The trip to the circus wasn't the right time to ask about it but I was curious as we drove through the town. We chattered like a barrel of monkeys on the way home, but Rita didn't say 'shut up' once. We'd all had a good time.

It was a crazy, happy time. Every visit we tried to introduce the boys to real life outside the camine and little things such as a pizza or an ice-cream filled them with delight. I noticed the one advantage the boys brought from the camine was their practical skills. Due to their enforced work regimes, there was little they couldn't tackle on their land. We paid a contractor to plough the garden and from then it was up to the lads to keep it planted and in good order. We visited as often as we could and always found Marianna was coping admirably. It was time to trust our boys to make a success of their new lives.

Gheorgie

*Rita and Eric took us to Iasi. I didn't like Iasi. I liked the trip
– all of us together was fun but I was scared in Iasi. I bet no one
has ever seen a bigger place in all the world. I didn't like the
noise. It gave me a headache. And so much traffic was like hell.
Umm...I like being with the animals at home best. Quietly. I
like sitting with them, feeding them and making sure they aren't
hurt. I could have stayed at home with Mariana but Dorin made
me go. He said Rita and Eric would be disappointed if I didn't
go but I thought they would be OK about it. Anyway, I never go
against what Dorin says, so I went.*

*We visited a restaurant in Iasi and Daniela came to meet us.
We hadn't seen her for ages. I like Daniela. She talks our
language and always wants to know if we have any problems.
Sometimes Rita talks in English and Daniela tells us in
Romanian 'cos Rita's Romanian is funny. We understand her
but she says things funny. When she has something serious to say
to us, she sits us down and makes us listen. If Dorin interrupts
(he always does that) she says, 'shut up' and he does. We have a
lot of respect for Rita and Eric 'cos they saved us from the camines
and gave us our house. Every Christmas we have a drink and
say 'Narok' to them for our new life. I'd like to see where they
live in England, but I wouldn't like the journey, so I can't go.
Even if Mariana gives me a pill, I still feel sick in a car, so I
don't think I'd like an aeroplane. That would be real scary.*

*When we got back home I was pleased I'd been 'cos lots of the
village kids wanted to know all about it. They'd never been so
far and wanted to know all about the moving staircase. Rita told
Mariana and Paul all about it when we got home and she
laughed about it all over again. I like it when she laughs. She
often gives me a hug and tells me I'm special. No one else ever
said I was special – only Rita. Everybody used to tell me I was
handicapped or mad when I was in a camine.*

166

Adrian

One year Rita and Eric took us for a day out in Iasi. We were excited. It's a long way to Iasi and we'd never been further than Birlad. They also said we could visit Daniela. We had a bit of money saved. I wanted to buy a new shade for our bedroom light, Dorin wanted some new jogging bottoms (he can't manage buttons or zips) and Gheorgie wanted an ice cream in a restaurant. He'd seen a pretty girl eating one on TV.

We all set off early. We had chosen what to wear the night before and it was our smartest clothes. The sort we wear if there is a wedding in the village. We never have to wear other people's clothes now. I can remember when I first realised that I had new clothes. I could hardly believe it. Nobody had ever worn them before me. I felt great. Mariana never makes us share what we wear, and the wardrobe is full of clothes, some for summer and some for winter.

It took a long time to get to Iasi and the roads were very bumpy until we were nearly there. Then I noticed there were new roads that were smooth and sounded soft under the wheels of the car. We had to stop in the forest to have a pee. Dorin is the worst. He always wants a pee, but Rita never seems to mind. Eric teases us. He says we're like three old men 'cos we need to pee so much!

We first saw Iasi from the top of a hill. I had never seen anything so huge. The buildings stretched for ever and there were some houses that must have cost a lot of money. They were like six of our house, all put together. Dorin kept asking about everything. He wants to know what everything costs. Eventually Rita told us to 'shut up.' She always says that when we keep talking and she can't think straight. We all understand the English words 'shut up'. She said it was like having three monkeys in the back of the car.

167

When we managed to park, Eric said we would go shopping first and afterwards we could go and look at the Palace of Culture and have a beer or an ice cream. I was thinking that maybe I would rather have a music CD than a lampshade by now, but I didn't know if I had enough money. The traffic was really noisy. I kept standing still just to look and Eric had to rescue me from being run down by the cars a couple of times. Gheorgie told me my mouth was wide open and I'd get a wasp caught in it if I wasn't careful. And there was a tram, too. It ran on lines with big electric cables on top. I'd never seen anything like it, not even on TV.

We went into a huge shop with an upstairs. It sold everything. Music machines, clothes, chairs, socks and even lottery tickets. We saw a huge moving metal thing with steps that kept appearing and before we had time to think Eric pushed us on it. I was all right. It made me laugh, but Dorin nearly had a fit. He wobbled and tried to get his balance and Rita grabbed hold of him and laughed so much she had tears on her face. Dorin said 'uppa,' but I knew he was scared. It takes a lot to scare Dorin but that scared him. It was moving up quite fast. The worst bit was at the top 'cos none of us knew how to get off. Rita shouted 'uppa' and grabbed Dorin. Eric gave me and Gheorgie a push and then we were off. If I'm honest, I was a bit scared, too, but I didn't show it. Rita said it was the funniest thing she'd seen in a long time and was still laughing when we started looking for Dorin's joggers.

We bought loads more than we came for – trainers for Dorin which are always tricky 'cos his feet aren't really feet at all, some new cushions for the house, six music CDs which I didn't have to use my money on and some batteries which Eric remembered we needed for the TV controller. By this time, we were feeling a bit tired. I think it was all the noise and new things to look at, but I felt as if I'd worked in the field all day and it wasn't even dinner time. I didn't say how I felt though 'cos I didn't want the day to end. I'd never even dreamed about a day like this.

Rita told us we were going to meet Daniela and have something to eat. I hadn't thought about food 'cos Mariana made sure we had a big breakfast, but as soon as it was mentioned I was hungry. I love eating in restaurants. I like hotdogs and pasta and meat.

Dorin

The first time we went to Iasi with Rita and Eric was great. We've been lots of time since, but the first time is the one I remember. I wanted to ask lots of questions, but Adrian told me to wait and see. Rita and Eric told us there would be lots of traffic, lots of shops and that we had to stay close so we would be safe. She didn't say what we would be safe from, but I thought maybe there were lots of gypsies there and they would try to steal from us. When they come to the village, everybody goes indoors and locks everything up.

I was a bit worried about the long journey 'cos I always need a pee. I know Eric never minds stopping for me, but it can be a bit embarrassing. Anyway – we stopped in the woods and Eric had a pee, too, so I felt better about it. It was a nice day, but it had rained overnight, and we had to scrape the mud from our shoes before we got back in the car.

I knew what Iasi looked like because I always watch the news and it's often on TV. There's a lot of crime in Iasi. People nick cars and things. I'd seen some very smart people, too, wearing suits and dresses. I suppose it was bigger than I thought it would be and the shops were huge. I didn't think they would sell so much stuff – not even in ten years. We went into the biggest shop of all. Rita said it was called a departmental shop, but I'd never heard of that. We went up a moving staircase. I was OK but

Adrian and Gheorgie were scared of it. Rita held on to me, but she didn't have to. I was OK.

We bought lots of stuff. Rita and Eric paid for everything and we didn't have to spend our own money. I don't think we had enough to buy very much anyway.

When we went to meet Daniela, I wanted to drink a beer with her. She comes to see us lots of times when Rita and Eric are in England and she's always kind to us. She asks us lots of questions, often the same ones each time she comes. Perhaps she forgets the answers.

Before we went home, we went to the fair. Now that was good. Lots of music; things moving around that made me feel dizzy and a smell that made me hungry. We had burgers, just like in films. Gheorgie wanted some pink fluffy stuff on a stick. He behaves like a kid sometimes. Adrian kept wandering off. No matter how often Eric told him to stay close, he didn't remember. Eric asked if we wanted a ride on something. I said no. What I was really thinking was that I'd like a ride on a roundabout. I wanted to sit in the fire engine but I could see it was for little kids. Rita said she would take us on the waltzers if we wanted. We all said no but now I wish we had 'cos I've never been to a fair since. I think we were scared. I wouldn't be scared now.

Adrian

One day Rita and Eric said we were going to Iasi again. I think Dorin needed some new clothes and Gheorgie had some birthday money to spend. I love going to Iasi, but this trip was different. We were going to meet Daniela, which is always nice. I love looking around her flat 'cos she has nice things and doesn't mind us looking. And we always go out for a pizza and a beer. I feel like a proper person when we go to a restaurant. The waiters have no idea I was in a camine and sometimes they even call me 'sir'.

This day Daniela said we were going to work with her. I knew she worked with street kids, so I was curious about what we were going to do. Dorin wanted to know everything, even before we set out. Daniela smiled and told him to wait and see.

We went in the car to another area of Iasi. First, I noticed lots of rubbish around and then we turned into a street where I was shocked. None of the buildings had any windows and there were black fire marks up the outside. Lots of kids were running around with no shoes and snotty noses. I hadn't seen kids like that since I left the camine.

Daniela said she had to go inside to see a boy who lived there. I offered to look after the car 'cos I thought it would have its wheels taken if we left it. Eric said he'd stay behind so that I could go inside. He'd been there before.

Inside there were no stairs and Daniela said all the wood had been burnt to keep the people warm. Lots of people were squatting around the walls. They were sitting on piles of rags 'cos there was no furniture. There was a smell of burnt wood and poo. They didn't have a lavatory, I suppose.

Dorin kept talking and talking. He wanted to know everything. Daniela told us that she visited the building a lot and there were three children living there who she had managed to get to school. One had stopped going, so she wanted to see if there was a problem.

We waited while she asked around about the boy. Someone said he didn't live there anymore. I could see it worried Daniela. She found a man sitting on a window ledge and had a long conversation with him and then she got cross. She was telling him she had to speak to the boy. I think the man was his father. After a while the man jumped down off the window and took Daniela out into the street. Rita said we could follow her.

We found the boy. He was in another burnt-out house, curled up in a corner with a dog. When Daniela spoke to him, he didn't *want to get up. She made him and he had a black eye, bruises all over his chest and he couldn't move his arm. Daniela was threatening the man with the police. She was furious. You don't want to tangle with Daniela when she's furious! After a few minutes she told the father she was taking the boy to hospital. The father shouted that she should mind her own business. He said he hoped she had money to pay the hospital 'cos she'd get nothing from him.*

The boy had a broken arm and it was plastered up. Daniela had to pay for it but I think I saw Eric give her money. There was a lot of discussion about what to do with the boy.

Daniela said she would take him to the Joseph house where he would be looked after until his arm was better. She said she would go back another day to see his father. I bet he got a good telling off from her. She said parents aren't allowed to beat their kids 'cos there is a law to protect them. I was surprised about that. I guess it didn't apply to camines.

Then we went shopping.

For many years Dorin had expressed an interest in his birth family. He had vague details gained from the director of the camine and he knew his family lived in Vaslui. Each time Daniela visited the village he asked her if she would help him find them. It was a curiosity rather than a desire to live with them, as he was very settled and happy in the house. Daniela eventually discussed the possibility with Eric and me and told us that his family address was on the paperwork she received when he left the camine.

We gave it a lot of thought and couldn't decide if it would be in his best interests, so it was put on hold while we thought about it further. I also worried what effect it might have on the other two if Dorin's family became a reality. However, in the spring of 2008 when I made the trip to Giurcani with my younger son Robert, who had just become a trustee of the charity, Dorin was insistent that we take him to find his family.

We asked Daniela if she would talk to Dorin and be sure he understood the worst-case scenario; we worried he may be rejected on the doorstep. As an adopted child who searched for and found her birth mother, (that introduction was made on a doorstep too,) I was well aware of the urges he was experiencing. I didn't have the heart to refuse him. And so, we set off one day, taking Daniela with us to translate.

His family lived in a high-rise apartment in Vaslui and we picked our way up the dark and dirty concrete stairwell, taking care over broken steps and avoiding the litter blown in by the biting wind. Dorin was ahead of us all, clearly a man on a mission; my heart and head were full of trepidation for him.

The door of the apartment was opened by a young woman who told Daniela her mother was out in the town shopping. She had a face so like Dorin's that it left me in no doubt we had found the right family. Daniela clearly didn't believe the girl and went to great lengths to explain that we were not a debt collector or anyone bringing bad news. She went on to tell the girl that we had brought Dorin to see the family. She elaborated that he didn't want anything from them – just to meet them. Eventually the mother poked her head around the door and invited us in.

The reunion was poignant, for Dorin and for me. Dorin's mother was clearly emotional to see him. She put her arm around him and peered at him as if she was short-sighted. I don't know whose heart was beating the loudest in that room. The air was charged with emotion you could taste.

His mother explained to Dorin that she'd been given no choices when she gave birth to a deformed baby. She and her husband were living with her mother-in-law at the time and much pressure was brought to bear to get rid of Dorin. Everyone was indoctrinated under Ceausescu to treat children with imperfections as unacceptable; it was the law that they were hidden away in camines. Such children had no place in the dictator's scheme to build a 'perfect race' which he pursued with all the vehemence of Hitler. Dorin's mother told us she'd fought her mother-in-law and husband for as long as she could, but eventually, when she became pregnant again Dorin had to go away.

We were served coffee in a very clean and welcoming home. There were two sisters in the house that day, a husband to one of them and two small babies. They chatted to Dorin with a friendliness that was heart-warming. His mother produced a box of photos and showed us one of Dorin as a baby. When he was two years old, she explained, the family forced her to take Dorin to Giurcani. Here he was left to the tender mercy of the state system, but she visited him for a while, making the long journey as often as she could. As her family grew, she found it impossible to travel the distance to Giurcani. She told us she'd eventually divorced her drunkard husband and brought her family up as a single mother, happy to be away from the influences of him and her mother-in-law.

Daniela told her Dorin was now living in his own house with two friends and that Eric and I were responsible for him for his lifetime. She appeared relieved that he now had a happy life. When we left there were promises made to stay in touch with him which were sadly broken. The sisters told Dorin they would visit from time to time but when they failed to materialise, Dorin took it all in his stride. He wrote them off in typical Dorin style. 'If they don't want anything to do with me then I don't want to see them either.' It is impossible to know his true feelings, but I think he has fed that deep longing to know his roots and is happy with the life he has.

Chapter 17

'I sometimes wondered, if I had a Dad, would he beat me?'

Adrian - survivor of the camine in Giurcani

I have been privileged to enjoy many family occasions in the village with people I've become attached to over the years. Probably the most colourful and exciting are Romanian weddings which are richly textured and offer a feast of mammoth proportions together with traditional music for dancing. Alcohol is at the centre of the celebration. These typically Latin-style, exuberant affairs often last for two or three days. There is much singing and dancing into the early hours of the mornings and huge amounts of food and drink are consumed.

The wedding service takes place in the village church and in Giurcani the bride and groom walk to church together, stopping to receive good wishes on the way. Most of the families walk behind and there is a real sense of occasion. On arrival at the church, (Russian Orthodox) the bride and groom are led in circles around the altar and the priest does a lot of chanting of prayers while wafting pungent incense around with gusto. There are very few seats in Romanian churches and most people stand to watch the service. Crowns are placed on the heads of the newly-weds and then prayers said for a long and happy life together. There is an exchange of rings at some point in the service, too.

Probably less spectacular, but still of interest for westerners, are the Orthodox funerals. Much importance is placed on family and friends viewing the body in an open casket and flowers are placed around it. Often, caskets are carried around the town on trucks or carts with the bodies displayed amid a profusion of flowers. Black clothes are worn as a mark of respect and many women wear veils over their faces. I noticed that for both weddings and funerals, kudos is given to the family if the occasion is attended by foreigners.

I have also had the good fortune to visit many different areas of Romania over the last thirty years. It is a beautiful country, but its crowning glory must be the Carpathian Mountains which sprawl from east to west. They contribute to difficult journeys when trying to reach Giurcani overland, but their beauty in all seasons is remarkable.

Eric and I have travelled in and out of Romania by just about every type of transport possible. We've flown into Bucharest and taken the dreary train journey to Birlad more times than we can remember. We've twice travelled overland by motorbike and taken our car about four times. Latterly, we took our motorhome which created huge excitement in the village. In recent years it has been possible to fly directly to Iasi and from there we pick up a hire car. All our trips have been interesting, some scary and some exciting.

177

One journey I remember well is the first time we rode out on the motorbike. My husband was very proud of his succession of BMW touring bikes, a habit acquired in the police force, and they made a comfortable ride for me. On one occasion we scooted through Europe without a hitch until we came to the Romanian border post at Oradea where we met the usual chaos. There were hundreds of people mingled with a serpent of cars, lorries and vans winding around the roads, all trying to squeeze into the country. The visa and checkpoint personnel were some of the most corrupt, lazy and rude people I'd ever met. They were blatant about their expectations of money, cigarettes or other luxury goods if you wished to spend less than six hours waiting to pass through. The wait for the uninitiated, or those unable to proffer bribes, could be all day – anything up to fourteen hours. Over the years we have learnt to put aside our good intent to never condone bribes, and each trip we head to the front of the queue. Anyone on English plates was gazed at in awe and our spoken English, our smart BMW motorbike and Eric's retired police ID always did the trick. There were enough other issues in Romania to riddle me with guilt and I refused to allow those episodes to become one of them.

On this occasion we stayed in a hotel about ten miles inside the Romanian border where there was no garage space available for the bike. We knew the risks if we left it unattended, particularly overnight. Good locking systems would be no deterrent to thieves and the chances of having a bike to continue the journey the next day, were slim. But the friendly man on the reception desk told us that for ten US dollars a member of staff would guard the bike all night. This looked like a good option, so the man was paid, and we promised him a tip in the morning if he did a good job. And indeed, the bike was safe.

We set off after a good breakfast on a glorious spring day for the anticipated ride through the Carpathians. I am our designated photographer and always carry a small camera on the back of the bike from where I've achieved some of my best photos. I remember I was awed by the glorious scenery, the trees bursting with life in every imaginable shade of green. The deep pine forest made way for deciduous woodland and the wildflowers were a profusion of colour, matched only by the costumes of the many gypsy women we saw along the way.

As we travelled, we noticed signs of house building. A good omen we felt – a suggestion that the economy was improving. In the poorer areas the new homes were constructed of traditional mud and straw although people who could afford modern methods of blocks or brick were also hard at work. Since the death of Ceausescu, village people had been given pieces of land to enable them to make a new start to their lives.

As evening drew near, Eric announced a fuel stop was required before looking for somewhere to stay. The petrol station was easy to find, and we duly pulled in and fuelled-up. There was discussion between the garage staff and Eric about which fuel should be put into the bike. My Romanian vocabulary didn't run to defining different grades of fuel and all the pumps had black hoses. Eventually, our needs were decided by the guy on the pumps and we set off into an amazing sunset.

179

As the rosy glow in the sky gradually turned to a crimson fire, I tapped Eric on the shoulder to ask if he would stop for me to takes photos. There was a silence from the front. I peered around his helmet and asked if he'd heard my request. A sharp voice called back, 'If I stop, we'll never get going again. I've got the wrong fuel in the bike and she's coughing like hell.' Never one to notice the finer points of an engine, I'd been oblivious to his anxious concerns for the last fifty miles or so. He decided to keep the bike going until the fuel was low and then top up with the right petrol. I never got my sunset photos and we travelled well into the night, stopping only when we found a rare, all-night garage. Luckily, the wrong fuel had been taken when the bike was still half full, and we hoped the mixture of the two fuels would see us through. It did. The thought of being marooned in the wilds of the Carpathians didn't sit easily and I couldn't get the thought of our near miss out of my mind for weeks.

We again travelled to Romania by motorbike in August 2004. My younger son Robert married Katherine in the beautiful Cardinham church in Cornwall on a glorious, blue-sky day. We set off after the celebrations, happy and thrilled for our newly-weds. We were also full of anticipation for our bike trip through Europe.

All bikers learn the art of travelling light and we were no exception. We allowed ourselves just one pannier of belongings each – all light-weight summer clothes on this occasion as Romanian summers can reach 40 degrees. It was Eric's first summertime visit to Giurcani and with the expectation of wall-to-wall sunshine, he packed accordingly. We could not have foreseen the events to come.

Our journey to Giurcani was glorious. Romania unfolded further layers of her amazing countryside to us for there is always something new to see in that fascinating country. I remember the Gypsy Kings' houses with roofs shining silver in the sunlight, their colourful paintwork and ornate gardens unlike anything I'd seen elsewhere. As ever, we saw poverty throughout the journey, especially in the villages where small children waved from rutted roadsides as we flew through the Carpathians. There is something magical about motorbike riding – smells fill your senses until you are bursting with the amalgamated flavours of the world.

As expected, we had a lovely time with the boys and spent most of our days buying yet more essentials, painting the house again with the help of the boys and watching Marianna make light work of bottling and preserving the harvest of peppers, cucumbers, tomatoes and plums. She was a wizard at providing for her family and the boys.

Something that made my heart sing during that visit was how well the villagers had accepted the lads. We had no reports from Marianna of theft or unpleasantness and we saw that an easy relationship existed when the boys were around the village. Another worry had been put to bed.

Over the early years of the boy's independence, we became aware that certain aspects of their skills-training were not making progress. Cooking was one omission and I never saw them wash any clothes.

When we asked the boys to demonstrate what they had learned, particularly how their skills in the kitchen had developed, we learned from Dorin that the boys were taking their meals with the family. Likewise, Marianna was doing the boy's washing and house cleaning. At first, I was disappointed. This was not setting the boys on the road to independence; however, we could see they had created such a strong bond and happy lifestyle with the Manole family, we were reluctant to intervene.

When Daniel Manole finished university, he had returned to live with his parents and added another level of care and a further role model for the boys. Daniel married his beautiful wife Alina, shortly after he graduated, and she too was happy to embrace our boys. We felt as if we had won the lottery.

Over time, we discovered our lads were being treated by Marianna as family i.e. men were cooked for and excused from all domestic chores. The pay-off from them was the work they did on the land; not only their own, but they worked the Manole ground, too. Having promised myself in the early years that I would always listen to local ways and customs, I had to agree the system worked well for them all.

On this particular summer visit Dorin told us, in no uncertain terms that the house needed plastic windows. Apparently, two houses in the village had installed them and he coveted them with a vengeance. He'd spent time asking the owners every detail about their new acquisition. How much did they cost, were they 'good'? Where did they come from, could anyone have them? We told him he could leave them on his 'dream list' as we only had money for essentials. It appeared to satisfy him, for that year at least.

The village roads threw dirt in our faces as is usual during summer months. I had forgotten just how bad it could be, particularly on the motorbike. It feels as though your eyes, nose and mouth are constantly full of grit and it's not unusual to develop a dry cough. But we had a good time.

We stayed with our friends Didi and Tori and got involved in the life of the village. Every-time we returned to Giurcani we had to make a dozen or so house-visits to catch up with different families, all of whom had offered us kindness and hospitality over the years. Everyone wanted to hear our news and tell us bits of gossip from around the community. Each year there had been a wedding or a birth. Often, there had been more than one funeral. Children had grown and many gone off to college, much to the pride of their parents. We always visited the camine children, too.

The family gave us good reports on the boys. A little concern was expressed about Adrian drinking too much wine, but it was nothing the family couldn't deal with, they assured us. I was pleased to see that Daniel and Alina's relationship with the boys was easy and friendly too. Daniela, as usual, came to the village to see us.

After a wonderful two weeks we eventually said our goodbyes. We set off on the long journey home, pleased to be travelling in the wonderful summer weather. I love travelling by motorbike – the hippy in me would eulogise about 'communing with nature.' Eric would just say it was fun. However, when we reached the Carpathian Mountains we were met with torrential downpours of rain. It was a particular worry for Eric as having a pillion passenger adds to problems in bad weather. The rain was relentless for hours.

We were at the point of deciding to wait out the weather, hoping to find a small cafe or kindly family who would offer us shelter. As we debated what course of action would be the safest, we came upon yet another faceless village where villagers were standing in the middle of the road, causing Eric to stop. We surveyed the scene and realised the road had disappeared before our eyes. A huge chunk of the village street had been washed away by the rain.

We dismounted and joined the group of villagers who parted in amazement to see a UK registered bike and two, sodden, leather-clad strangers in their remote village. I asked if there was an alternative route but received the familiar shrug suggesting they had no idea what I had asked. Many villages have strong rural dialects and my stumbling Romanian appeared to be Double Dutch to them.

Eric told me that he would try to find a way around the flood water with the bike and suggested I tried to cross the gaping hole in the earth. We hoped to meet up on the other side. As he disappeared down a muddy side road that was not yet affected by the flood water, I asked a couple of guys if they would help me cross the hole. A lady never feels at her best in biking leathers and helmet, and the drowned-rat appearance certainly undermined my self-confidence. Luckily, husband and wife were reunited within ten minutes and both were in one piece. We did make it home unscathed, but it wasn't the sun-drenched journey we had expected. We later learned of the devastating floods in Prague and

Venice that damaged so many rare works of art that summer.

Eric's desire to help the Joseph Foundation with a fostering programme was not forgotten and it got off to a flying start thanks to the Rotary Club in the Isles of Scilly. Enough money was generated to pay for Daniela to place and supervise many foster children in the villages surrounding Iasi. He gave regular reports of progress to the Rotary Club and they agreed to provide each child with a gift at Christmas. We made several visits to the foster families with Daniela and realised the Joseph Foundation in Iasi was, yet again, leading the way with another ground-breaking idea.

As the crisis of Romania's children slipped to the back burner in world terms, money became harder to find. Diminishing funds at the Joseph Foundation affected Daniela's life as both her wages and the overheads of the Joseph Foundation house relied on donations. A further blow was the Romanian government's decision to ban international adoption in two thousand and five. Suddenly, the situation was not so rosy.

In two thousand and six the money to run the Foundation dried up, (as a direct result of the ban on foreign adoptions,) and the Foundation directors were forced to put the children into foster homes. It was a sad time as Eric's donations became a mere drop in the ocean. The house was sold and the majority of staff lost their jobs. Luckily, Daniela managed to stay on the meagre payroll in a city centre office which was maintained to assist when it could with crisis care of street children. For my part, I couldn't believe private enterprise of such a high standard could slip away without trace. But it did.

The Foundation continued to pay foster families a small allowance to take the children into their homes. The money barely covered the costs of each child, deliberately small in order to identify those families with a genuine desire to help. But eventually, Daniela told us that there was no longer money to pay them and she feared the children would be turned out on to the street again.

Eric approached the Isles of Scilly Rotary Club again and with typical generosity, they agreed to back our rescue plan. They offered to pay the foster fees for all the children for one full year and Daniela was able to keep the children safe for a while.

.

Chapter 18

Over the years we developed a close and enduring friendship with two village families; the Rotaru family and the Manole family who have both been an incredible source of inspiration and support to us. They have opened their homes and their hearts to Eric and me, and also to our friends who have visited the village. Didi was, until he retired, the head teacher at the local primary school. When government funding became available to build a new school in the year two thousand, he stayed in post for an extra year to oversee the transfer of the pupils into the new building. (happily for me, the school was built inside the vastly expensive metal fence which charity money had purchased, many years before.) Didi was a keeper of bees, a sculptor of wood and metal and an archaeologist of country-wide renown. (He has, in recent years written several books on his Roman finds which have been published under his name Marin Rotaru.) His collection of antiquities was acquired through hard work and dedication and in the early years of my visits it was a common sight to watch him disappear over the grassy hillsides on his small, pop-pop motorcycle with a canvas bag slung over his shoulders. He had enjoyed his hobby, digging for Roman artefacts, since his early twenties and amassed an amazing museum of pieces which, until the new school was built, were housed in glass cabinets in the old classrooms. His house always displayed Roman pots and metal objects, many lovingly restored.

About ten years ago Didi asked if we would sponsor the production of a bi-annual, archaeology magazine which he intended to write and illustrate, mainly to document his collection of treasures. This we did for a couple of years and he created a work of art by drawing bones and ancient artefacts with a fine-nib pen. It took him many months, but he was delighted when his knowledge and findings appeared in print and subsequently became noticed by influential people. He received the recognition and funding he deserved. These days, he is called upon to lecture in Bucharest and other towns and many of his artefacts have been loaned to museums.

Didi's talent for creating works of art from wood, stone and metal are displayed around his home and garden. All are museums in their own way. Our home, also, displays lovely gifts made by his skilled hands. If ever there was someone who flourished after the fall of communism, then he is the perfect example. He's a humble man with a multitude of talent.

In the early years of my visits Tori was the local banker in the village and she ran the branch of CEC Bank from her front room. It was weird to wake at 7.30am to hear the financial dealings of the village carried out on the other side of my bedroom wall! Now retired, she and Didi keep extraordinarily busy with their bees and land which they still cultivate. They are also proud grandparents.

The Manole family are the other important people to us. When they were recommended by Didi and Tori as 'good people' it was our great fortune and their generosity of spirit that allowed us to make our dreams for the boys a reality. They were indeed 'good'. Paul, Mariana, their son Daniel and his wife Alina care for the boys in a way we could never have dreamed about. Lavinia was the first grandchild of the family and she already had the boys wrapped around her little finger. Alex arrived three years later.

I considered Mariana and Paul to be courageous when they took on the enormous risk of caring for the boys. It was a ground-breaking scheme with no guarantee of success. We always knew it was not only a monetary decision as they demonstrated a genuine desire to change the boys' lives. Sadly, some villagers, as expected, were not supportive. Much was said, we learnt later, to dissuade Mariana from taking the risk. People tried to fill her head with negative thoughts which made her determination on behalf of those boys, even more remarkable. But she held her nerve and has been a shining example of what can be done with the right attitude and a little faith.

In recent years the responsibility for Dorin, Adrian and Gheorgie has passed to Daniel and Alina who are the next generation in the Manole family. Although Paul and Mariana have retired, they keep busy with the animals and vegetable gardens and Mariana still does much of the cooking for the family. The relationship they now have with the boys is one of grandparents, which gives Adrian, Dorin and Gheorgie another layer of proxy family.

189

When we appointed Paul and Mariana it was agreed that we would pay them a salary for two years but continue to support the boys for life. Over the years we have been able to reduce the money we give the family although the boys will never be totally self-sufficient. There will always be a need for hospital bills to be paid; medicines and winter wood are expensive, and the upkeep of the house still falls to us. We will always help the Manole family if times get tough, because they are the mainstay of our boys' lives. Due to hard work on the boy's part, and trust from the Manole family, we think we have created the perfect partnership.

If the boys lived in a town, I believe we would have set them up with a small business. We had many ideas but were unable to bring them to fruition in such an isolated community. Originally, we wanted to set up a small cheese-making business. Daniel had some good ideas for starting the business after he graduated and there was some initial success, however two obstacles appeared. Firstly, the government brought in strict EU legislation regarding food preparation, which imposed massive amounts of red tape. Secondly, an exceptionally hot summer and two very harsh winters wiped out the grassland needed for the cows, so little milk was produced.

We looked at starting a small shop, a shoe repair business and breeding and selling goat meat. (This also fell under the demanding auspices of EU regulations.) We eventually had to accept that in the wilds of the countryside there is little but self-sufficiency. Even Daniel, with his university degree, cannot find work in

Giurcani. But we are not downhearted as the boys stay fully occupied.

An interesting aside to the Manole's trust and confidence all those years ago, is the number of families in Giurcani who have since fostered camine children. In many respects, Marianna and Paul blazed a trail that others followed. The families all receive a pittance from the government for a fostering programme which was instigated after the closure of the camines, although it must be said, not all placements are good. Some families took the children purely on monetary grounds and I fear for the conditions they endure. Conversely, I have seen many happy outcomes too. There never appears to be a checking system of any sort, but I could be wrong about that.

The third person to deserve our accolades is Daniela Cornestean. Without her it would have been impossible to tell this story. We were lucky enough to meet a highly intelligent lady, a qualified psychologist and fluent English speaker and someone we've grown to love. However, despite her many talents, her adult life teetered on a knife-edge in the early years, due to the tough life in Romania. When we first met her, she was poorly paid and often had insufficient money to buy the basics of life. Her work for the various charities in Iasi was commendable but as she explained to us, 'it's not who you are but who you know that gets you the best jobs in Romania'. However, slowly life has improved for her and she now owns her own apartment, has a job she enjoys and is secure for life. Thankfully, we no longer need to worry about Daniela.

When the boys had been living in their new house for about a year, I received an unexpected email from a Dutch lady called Hannah. She had been to Giurcani and met the boys and was impressed with our project. Her main question was, *'would you share the blueprint of how you released the boys?'* She thought she could raise money in Holland to create a similar project. Eric and I were thrilled to think that more of the camine children would have a chance of a better life. We corresponded for a few days and I explained how we had achieved getting the boys released and any other information I thought would be helpful. Her plan was to build a house in the village and take nine children out of the camine. We agreed to meet up the next time we visited.

Over the coming months Hannah kept me up to date on her progress. She had managed to persuade the authorities to donate a piece of land on the edge of the camine for her to build the house, which got under way within a few months. Her aim was to find useful employment for the children in her care. I had concerns about that coming to fruition as we had taken the three most able lads and after all our efforts, failed to get them into paid work. I kept my opinions to myself as she clearly had people on board to help her.

I was impressed with this Dutch lady and when we eventually met, my opinion didn't change. Eric and I could see she was driven by a passion to help the camine children and she spent months in the village getting the house built. She was kind to our three boys too and visited them with small gifts. For the next couple of years, we heard much of Hannah's progress.

It was clear to us that her project had many differences from ours but was driven by a similar ethos. Scale was the first obvious difference, as Hannah took nine boys, many from among the least able children in the camine. She chose some who, in my view, were unlikely to thrive in an independent project and others I had worked closely with and knew deserved the opportunity. Hannah entered into a contract with the Director in Vaslui to ensure her department paid the wages for a woman to cook and clean for the children. As with our lads, no adult would live in the house with them. I was delighted and wished her well. I knew her heart was in the project and she was well-funded.

And it worked for a while. Hannah taught some of her kids to weave cloth which she sold in Holland. They achieved great things and for me, it was a revelation to see the progress of children with such pronounced disabilities. They were all taught to work on the goat farm she set up and bicycles were provided for them to get to work. We were amazed how those less able kids responded to support. Suddenly, there was a community of camine children living in the village and any village prejudice appeared to be left behind.

One day we had bad news via our skype link with the boys. They told us that after about three years of funding and care, Hannah's project became too expensive to support. The money just ran out. I know this gave Hannah sleepless nights and after much heart-searching, she gave the house and the children back to the state. Some children still live in the house today but the less able have gone to live with families in the village.

193

Over the years Eric and I stayed in touch with Hannah, and she continued to visit the village. One day I had an email from her telling us the water situation in the village had reached crisis point. The water source was so full of harmful minerals that no one could drink it and she wanted to bring a fresh supply into the village via a series of standpipes down the main street. This was a *déjà vu* moment for me, having watched the French attempt to do the same thing, without success, many years before.

Hannah asked us to contribute to the project, which created a dilemma for Eric and me. We have always taken the financial decisions of our work very seriously - using donated money is a massive responsibility. So, what to do now? I had been aware for some time that a water crisis in the village was imminent and we had even persuaded the Rotary Club in Iasi to attempt to bring a new source to the village several years before. Their experts had not found a way to do it.

Eric and I talked at length about the problem. Of course, water is the lifeline of every community on earth and in my mind, no one deserved it more than Giurcani. But I was anxious not to throw good money into a project that we had no control over. I knew that this was a complex problem with a high likelihood of failure. I was, however, impressed that Hannah was willing to try.

After much discussion we eventually reached a compromise. We told Hannah we would contribute to her project but only when the water supply was in and working successfully. We also wanted, as part of the agreement, a water pipe laid directly on to the boys' land so that we could provide a proper bathroom for them. Hannah agreed to our terms and work started on the hillside to find the precious water.

Another visit to the village was called for when Hannah announced the job was done. I was full of admiration for this woman who had worked against the odds to squeeze clean water from a deep well that had been drilled in a remote hillside many times before. Of course, she hadn't been personally involved in the digging, but I was under no illusions that without her, water would never have been found.

Our arrival in the village to inspect the new water supply was met with unbridled joy from Dorin who couldn't wait to show us their personal water pipe. True to her word, Hannah had organised water directly into the boys' house and we could now create a bathroom for them. We arranged to make the agreed donation to Hannah and the village was full of praise for her.

We arranged for a bath, basin and electric immersion heater to be fitted into a small extension we'd created years before. And hey presto – the lads had indoor facilities. But as always, there was a lot to do. It was decided the outdoor loo needed moving again, so Eric and the boys started digging the new hole and constructed a wooden shed over it with a wooden seat. Dorin insisted they had a sheepskin cover for the seat – ready for the winter months!

We were continually impressed by the relationship between the boys and the Manole family. Mariana cooked twice a day for all, and the fruits of her labour were visible in the faces of our chubby boys. There was a reciprocal arrangement in place whereby their good fortune was repaid by working hard for the family on their land.

When we asked Daniel what was needed for the future, he told us more animals would be essential to support the boys. To that end we launched a 'Sponsor a Sheep or a Cow' campaign when we returned to Scilly. Yet again, we had a wonderful response and sent enough money to purchase various animals.

Each year the boys' needs became less, which was good for us as we were both feeling a little 'fund raising weary.' We'd reached the age of retirement and in 2006 we decided, with many reservations, that the time had come to relocate from the Isles of Scilly to the mainland. Grandchildren were sprouting like asparagus stalks and we were anxious to have more access to them than was possible from Scilly. Eric's elderly parents were unwell and their futures uncertain.

And so, with regrets, we packed up our belongings and moved to beautiful Totnes where we put down roots. We continued to visit Romania every other year, but with the technical advances available we were able to skype the boys often. Dorin always had something he wanted but there was little he needed. Their lives had changed beyond recognition and we were so proud of our lads for their courage and ability to live amongst the people who had done them harm. When we see them invited to big outdoor lunches to celebrate a birthday or a saint's day, my heart swells with emotion that they accept their place at the table as if they were born to it.

In May 2012 we visited Giurcani, hoping for good weather. It was the first year we planned to take our campervan overland and intended to visit Croatia and Italy after spending time with the lads.

When we arrived in Giurcani we found the boys in good spirits. Dorin had, without doubt, put on even more weight, Adrian had a few more wrinkles, but so did we, and the family were fit and well.

Daniel told us that the previous winter had been a hard one for the boys. Snow had come early and it had crept through the ill-fitting wooden windows. Dorin elaborated that it had been bitterly cold in the house and it was now time for his plastic windows. We talked about the cost with Daniel and agreed that action was needed to keep the fabric of the house in good condition. To our amazement, within five days we saw the windows measured, ordered, delivered and fitted. Dorin could not have been happier, and we could not have been more surprised by the speed of it all.

The fitting of plastic, double-glazed windows in Romania was a revelation. Having bought some for our own home a few years earlier, we expected to order and pay for them and then ask the family to oversee the fitting some weeks after we left Romania. But it was not so. The windows were measured within two hours of our enquiry and duly fitted within four days. And the fitters came to do the job armed with a chainsaw. I watched Eric shake his head in consternation as they proceeded to cut the wooden windows out and 'tidy up the hole' with the chainsaw. The fabric of the house is basically mud and straw, so on reflection we realised it was an efficient method of working. Sadly, the fitters had no plan to make good the damage inside the house, so Daniel and Eric were called upon to clear up behind them. With a little help from everyone, the damage was repaired.

Dorin considered the project a triumph. He insisted, his ideas were always good although it took us a little time to appreciate it! We felt it was money well spent and had peace of mind that the following years would see the boys snug again.

Chapter 19

Over the years we have come to know each boy in a more intimate way than was possible when they lived in the camine. We recognise their strengths and make allowances for things they are unable to achieve. The strongest personality is Dorin and when we are at home in the UK, I imagine he spends hours compiling a list of 'essentials' which he keeps in his head until we visit. His is always the first voice we hear when we arrive. Dorin takes a keen interest in village politics which in Romania is a serious affair. He is vociferous during elections for the local mayor and has strong views when national elections take place. Although he doesn't have a vote, due to his disability, he holds court about the merits, and otherwise, of each candidate. I think he learns it all from television programmes and he is more than prepared to air his preferences to anyone who will listen. There is little he doesn't have an opinion about.

When he moved into the new house, there was one little luxury from his list that we allowed him. Dorin wanted a wooden bench outside the garden fence, and he wanted it badly. Amid all the budgeting for the essentials we had a little voice in our ear constantly asking for a seat. As life in a Romanian village is spent mainly outdoors during the summer months, we could understand why a little bench to sit on and watch the world go by was important for them. Most houses have wooden benches on the roadside and the world is put to rights on summer evenings by the more senior of the village while children play in the road. So, we relented and added a table and parasol for good measure. Oh, how happy Dorin was. A good deal of posturing and chatter took place as the boys attempted to establish their place in local society.

Adrian and Gheorgie are different from Dorin; both have a quieter and more diffident personality. I believe Gheorgie had a request, too, when they moved into the house – he wanted a swing in their new garden. It was provided with good grace and he and many others have spent happy hours on it.

Adrian is the master of disappearing and no one is ever sure where he's been. We worry that villagers give him wine which is not good when you are epileptic. When we took bicycles over one year, it was agreed Daniel would decide when they could use them as he needed to know where Adrian was. Poor Dorin is never going to ride a bike because of his physical challenges but we made it up to him in other ways. There is never any jealousy between the boys, and they are incredibly appreciative of everything done for them.

I like to think the horrors of the camine don't linger in their heads these days and it's notable that they rarely mention it. Astonishingly, they have even been known to invite the camine director in for a drink at Christmas. Maybe, I should take note of the boy's ability to put the past behind them, for I have never been able to forgive her for the obstructions she threw at our efforts to improve life for the children. Maybe I will work on that. Sadly, she lost her husband in two thousand and ten and it happened in a most horrible way. Sandu, who was a lovely kind man, tried to hook a chicken out of an old well but over-balanced and fell head-first into the water. By the time he was discovered he had drowned.

Adrian, Dorin and Gheorgie's new life has been played out in the same village where they suffered poverty, starvation and neglect throughout their childhood. Every day they meet the women responsible for their previously miserable existence but, amazingly, their troubled past has been put aside and they show an unwillingness to apportion blame for the cruelty and deprivation they suffered as children. They are too busy with their new lives and we see them laughing and joking with the women who caused them so much heartache; they even accept invitations into their homes. Maybe their generosity of spirit can be attributed to a blunted emotional awareness, or as a direct result of their lower IQ. Who knows? They have an uncanny knack of moving their lives forward and it's this, I believe, more than anything that has allowed them to meld to the normality of village life. Importantly, they have earned the grudging respect of villagers; those who in the past never rated them above animals in outhouses, now acknowledge their existence and recognise them as human beings. The boys have a place in the pecking order of village life, albeit near the bottom. They have the distinction of owning their own home and land and they contribute to the society around them. And I'm bursting with pride for them.

Each time we visit we see happy and busy lads living life to the full. Most importantly, I believe they have each reached their potential, wherever that lies. They have a natural respect for the Manole family, and I see significant signs of affection shared between them all. These days the lads tend their land with pride; they toil under the summer sun and shovel snow in the winter, but now their labour is self-enhancing; They are proud of their achievements and have smiles as wide as a Romanian summer sky.

In 2012 Eric and I travelled to Giurcani to celebrate twenty-one years of supporting the village. I was touched to find the Manole family had arranged a party for us to which many village friends were invited. It was made extra special by the attendance of a few of the camine boys. Many had popped up in foster families around the village and they too were invited. It was strange to meet them as grown men. Some towered above me and all had facial hair and manly voices. I had taught some to walk and introduced them all to play and the sound of my voice, attempting to sing songs. Very strange indeed. It was a special evening with wonderful food and good company.

There can be no end to this story as 'our boys', even as you read this, are living their lives with zest and vigour. Their guardians and the next generation of the Manole family are wonderfully committed to them and I believe they will be their surrogate family for life. Eric and I are under no illusions that the boys are little saints – I'm sure they must be brought into line from time to time. But the Manole family deal with problems as they arise and rarely bother us with them.

What more could Eric and I ever have hoped for? We continue to fundraise on a low-key basis and visit as regularly as we can, but the long-term future of 'our boys' lies with our own children and the younger generation of the Manole family. We have deep faith in them all.

Five Years Later

In some ways much has changed and in others, nothing has changed at all. Our boys still live and work in their house and are pro-active with the various maintenance projects as required. From time to time we get emails to say the stove needs repair or the winter wood has been used, but with money from us and the hands-on approach of Daniel, it soon gets resolved. The lads work the land and as far as we can ascertain, the bounty is shared by all.

As Eric and I have taken retirement, so too have Marianna and Paul. Their son Daniel and his wife Alina now have legal responsibility for all three boys and the similarity in age between each of them gives us peace of mind for the future. The family have acquired a small monthly allowance for each boy and a pension will be paid to them in the future. This is encouraging and I believe it marks progress and gives kudos to the many fostering programmes that continue to multiply around the villages.

Each time we visit we are told about the return of camine children to the village. Those lost children who disappeared when Romania entered the EU are now, of course, fully grown adults and many live with foster families in Giurcani. I get called by Dorin to visit specific houses as he always knows about the new arrivals. I have had many happy reunions with those children who are now adults with special needs. At last, they have found a safe place to be. It must be noted, some placements in the village are more caring than others, but as far as I can tell, they are all kinder and safer than the camine.

It is bitter-sweet for me to see the kids I grew to love, as adults; many were from my original feeding programme. It's clear they will never live independently in the community, due to their disabilities, but I'm so happy they have breathing space and the chance to live the best life possible for them.

During our 2016 visit we had an extraordinary happening and Dorin could hardly wait to tell us the latest news. He had remembered I had a special affinity for a little boy called Livio, all those years ago. When I browse my photos, I see many were taken of me cuddling that child who was one of the small scraps in my salon. I fed, nurtured, loved and taught him to walk. Dorin was so happy to tell me of Livio's recent arrival in Giurcani and assured me we should visit him and his foster mother, who was one of the women I knew from the camine.

Eric and I duly made our way up one of the dirt side-roads and arrived, unannounced at the home of a lady called Tinka. After hugs for me and an introduction to Eric, she invited us inside to meet Livio who I calculated was now thirty-two years old. He had grown into a tall, good looking man but it was easy to see he had pronounced difficulties. I was unsure how much speech he had, and I was not hopeful he would understand our conversation or remember me. After a few minutes he reached out his hand which I took as an invitation to touch him. I gave him a hug and very quietly sang 'Row, Row, Row the Boat' to him while giving him close eye contact. There followed what I can only describe as an explosive moment when he lit up like a light bulb and started clapping his hands, dancing a stomping rhythm and humming the tune. It was so emotional to witness that moment. Somewhere, deep inside a disturbed young man, sat a seed of memory, a glimpse of happiness from the cuddles we shared and the songs we sang decades before. Something inside me was deeply moved that day. Dorin teased me for my tears and reminded me I'd said I never needed to cry again in Giurcani. Why is that lad always right? But what an immense reward I received from Livio – one I shall carry to my grave.

That same year we took the boys on holiday. We decided to visit Dracula's Castle in Transylvania and we stayed for two nights in a four-star hotel. How those boys loved their first sight of mountains and how well they behaved. We were so proud of them.

Eric and I spoke often and at length with both the trustees of the charity and Daniela about the status of the boy's house. When the property was purchased it was signed to the Joseph Foundation in Romania as foreigners couldn't legally own land at that time. This eventually changed, but Eric and I were unwilling to have ownership of the house in our names. A particular worry came, however, when Daniela told us the Joseph Foundation office in Iasi was due to close and the Foundation would be de-registered as a charity. Apart from making us very sad, it focused our minds on what should be done with the boy's house.

We had worked closely with the Manole family for sixteen years and had nothing but trust and admiration for them. We were happy that the money we gave them made their own lives a little easier while caring for the boys, for without them our lads would have been in dire straits. Over the years we'd made unannounced visits and never found anything different from the visits when we are expected. Life jogged along at village pace, it was unremarkable and quietly defined by the seasons.

As I was edging ever closer to my seventieth birthday with an unbelievable twenty-six years of involvement behind me, we both felt some changes were required to safeguard the boys. I often commented that each visit we made could be the last, although to date we are both still fit and well. And of course, we'll continue to visit while we are able. However, we felt there was a responsible path to forge to ensure the longevity of our work. To this end, it was agreed the house would be signed over to Daniel Manole with a proviso that it would always be kept for the boys in their lifetimes. As Daniel and Alina are younger than the boys, it will probably be Lavinia and Alexander, who will benefit. And we are happy with that. Daniel agreed with our decision and it only took a visit to a notary to get everything in place. Daniela, as ever, was there to translate and ensure the correct clauses were included.

In recent years we've seen a welcome change in our friend Daniela's life; it has been slow to evolve and as yet has not reached a definite conclusion, but it is a happy time for her. The change came in the form of Al, an American from Washington DC who came to Romania as a volunteer to support small charities with finance and planning. He spent time with the Joseph Foundation in Iasi and naturally, his path crossed with Daniela. She has taken him to meet her parents and she has visited Washington, but she tells me 'there is no hurry'. I suppose five years is not long in the grander scheme of things, but maybe one day they will formalise their relationship. Just like Cilla used to say, 'I want to buy a hat!

2020. Brexit and Covid….

What can be said about either, really? The village has covid 19 as I write this, and the boys have been made aware of hand washing and not mixing. However, I can have no peace of mind from afar. Brexit is done and dusted, for better or for worse and we await permission to travel.

We had a zoom call from the boys on Christmas Day which was all the more special as our own family were not able to be with us. This ghastly shielding has nothing to recommend it and we have no idea when we can next visit the boys. These days we take life as it comes and don't dwell too much on what we can't achieve.

Eric and I share enthusiasm for our home and garden, we adore our family and feel blessed to have ten grandchildren. Our surrogate sons in Romania are happy and cared for.

Happy days all round then.

Printed in Great Britain
by Amazon

84808731R00122